The **e**lementary **M**inimal **E**nglish **T**est

音声ダウンロード

牧 秀樹
西田 雛

小学生版

最小英語テスト（eMET）ドリル

小学生版

開拓社

まえがき

　「英語なんてゲームと同じ。」そんな思いで，このドリルを作りました。2020 年 4 月より，小学 5 年生と 6 年生の外国語活動が，正式な「英語」という教科になりました。英語を勉強の一つだと考えたら，途端にやる気がなくなるかもしれませんが，ゲームの一つだと考えれば，一発クリアーしてやろうかという気持ちになるかもしれません。このドリルは，そんな小学生の皆さんを思い浮かべながら作りました。小学校によっては，英単語を書くという練習をあまりしていないかもしれません。だからこそ，このドリルを使って，書く力をつけていただければと思います。

　音声を使って，1 回 3 分程度で終わる問題が，24 題収載されています。このドリルにある簡易テストは，最小英語テスト小学生版（The elementary Minimal English Test ＝ eMET）と呼びます。時間が最短の小学生向け英語テストだからです。eMET は，もともとは，大学生の英語能力を測定するために開発された最小英語テスト（The Minimal English Test ＝ MET）にその起源があります。

　MET は，理科の実験に使用する**リトマス紙**に似ています。短時間で，学習者の英語能力をだいたい測定できるという点においてです。

　MET はまた，陰山英男立命館小学校副校長・立命館大学教授の『**百ます計算**』や川島隆太東北大学加齢医学研究所教授の『**脳トレ**』にも似ています。短時間の簡単な作業を繰り返し行うことで，脳が活性化し，一定の英語能力の向上が見られるという点においてです。

　牧秀樹が岐阜大学地域科学部で過去 20 年間調査した結果，MET には，二つの機能があることが分かってきました。一つは，MET には，英語能力を測定する機能があること。MET の得点と，TOEIC 等の得点との間に相関があり，したがって，MET を 3 分使って受ければ，だいたい，TOEIC 等の得点を予測することができます。

　もう一つは，MET には，英語能力を向上させる機能があること。異なる MET をいくつも実施し，最初に実施した MET を再度実施すると，解答を見せていないにも関わらず，その得点が統計的有意に向上します。

　このドリルは，MET の二つ目の機能を使って，「ゲーム感覚で」みなさんの英語の力を上げるお手伝いをしようと，作られました。小学校の授業であれば，授業の最初の「帯」活動としても，有効に活用できるかもしれません。eMET の問題はすべての穴が埋められないことがよく起きるため，もっと穴埋めしたくなり，何回も挑戦したくなるという声も届いています。

　MET についてのより詳しい説明は，牧秀樹著『The Minimal English Test（最小英語テスト）研究』（2018）を参考にしていただきたいと思います。また，eMET については，西田雛（牧秀樹研究室卒業）の岐阜大学地域科学部卒業論文を参考にしていただき

たいと思います（Nishida (2023)）。西田による調査（2021年9月に中国陝西省の小学校において実施された）の結果，本ドリルの小学5年（4）（音声 Track 04）の問題（20点満点）の得点とその小学校の5年生2学期期末英語テスト得点（100点満点）との間に統計的有意な相関があることが分かりました。その予測式は，$y = 2.03x + 51.91$ で，x に自分が獲得した eMET の得点を入れてみれば，自分が今その小学校にいたら，だいたい何点くらい取れるかわかります。

　第1題目の問題をやっていただければ，これまで述べてきたことが実感できると思います。このドリルが，みなさんの遊び友達となってくれるといいなと思っています。

　本ドリルの英語音声は，マイケル・セビエ（Michael Sevier）氏による録音です。米国コロラド州出身，岐阜大学地域科学研究科修士課程卒業の英語母語話者です。修士論文の執筆には，もちろん，MET を使っています。マイケル・セビエ氏の協力に感謝するとともに，中国における調査に惜しみなく尽力してくれた大阪大学大学院博士課程所属の邱暁石氏と中国陝西省の小学校教諭の邱凡氏にも，心より感謝いたします。また，本ドリル改善への示唆に対し，岡本美紀子氏に感謝いたします。

　最後に，困難な時世の中，本書の出版を引き受けてくださった開拓社の川田賢氏に万謝いたします。

2023年5月　　牧 秀樹・西田 雛

目　次

eMET のやり方

　eMET は，英語の音声を聞きながら，単語を埋めるだけの簡単なテストです。英語の音声だけを聞いていれば，それほど速いとは感じませんが，いったんテストが始まると，突然，襲い掛かるように速く感じます。ですから，単語が，聞きとれなかったり，書ききれなかったりした場合は，あきらめて，すぐに，次の空所に移るようにしてください。そうしないと，一度に 3 つくらい空所が吹っ飛んでしまうことがあり，得点の低下につながってしまいます。

　1 題終わるごとに，次のページに日本語訳と解答があるので，答え合わせをしながら，書ききれなかった箇所を確認し，また，意味が分からなかった箇所も，同時に確認してください。

　本書には，合計 24 題の eMET があり，小学 5 年，小学 6 年の各学年で学ぶ内容を中心に作られています。空所に入る単語の文字数は，全て 4 文字以下にしてあります。ただし，空所と空所の間が広いバージョンと狭いバージョンがあります。それぞれ，12 題ずつです。当然，狭いバージョンの方が難しくなっています。

　どれだけ自分が伸びたかを測定するには，各バージョンにおいて，第 1 題目の eMET（小学 5 年（1））を複写しておいて，その第 1 題目の eMET だけは採点せず（つまり，答えを見ず），他の 11 題が終わってから，その複写した第 1 題目の eMET を行い，そこで，第 1 題目の eMET を 2 枚，同時に採点してください。何点伸びたかがはっきり分かります。

　では，いよいよ，次のページから，どうぞ，eMET で遊んでください。「英語なんてちょっとしたゲームだよ。」

第1章

eMET 広いバージョン問題

　この章には，問題が12題あります。各問題には，空所（　　　）があります。英語の音声を聞きながら，（　　　）の中に，4文字以下（最大で4文字）の英単語を入れてください。

　1題終わるごとに，答え合わせをすることができます。各問題の次のページには，その英文の日本語訳が，そして，その次のページには，解答が太字で示されています。

　答え合わせが終わったら，問題のページに戻り，点数を記入しておくことができます。

eMET 小学 5 年 (1) 問題

英語の音声を聞きながら, ( ) の中に, 4 文字以下 (最大で 4 文字) の英単語を入れてください。

1. Look at this photo.　This is my dog.

2. What's ($)^1$ name?　My name is Mary.

3. What sport do you ($)^2$?　I like tennis.

4. What color do you like?　I ($)^3$ blue.

5. Do you like stories?　Yes, I do.

6. ($)^4$ you have a ruler?　No, I don't.

7. What do ($)^5$ want for your birthday?　I want a red ($)^6$.

8. What day is it today?　It's Friday.

9. When is your birthday?　($)^7$ birthday is July 4th.

10. What season do you like?　I ($)^8$ summer.

11. How many CDs do you have?　I have twenty CDs.

12. ($)^9$ much is this bag?　It's 500 yen.

13. Can you do ($)^{10}$?　No, I can't.

14. What subject do you like?　I ($)^{11}$ math.

15. What do you want to study?　I ($)^{12}$ to study science.

16. What do you want to be?　(　　　　　　)^{13} want to be a singer.

17. What card do (　　　　　)^{14} have?　I have a baseball card.

18. What do (　　　　　)^{15} do every day?　I play in the park every
　　　(　　　　)^{16}.

19. Is he a magician?　No, he is not.

20. (　　　　　)^{17} time do you get up?　I get (　　　　　)^{18} at seven.

21. After school I eat lunch.　Then I play with (　　　　)^{19} friends.

22. She is a farmer.　She can sing well.

23. (　　　　)^{20} is a teacher.　He is good at baseball.

24. Wash (　　　　)^{21} hands.　Don't push.

eMET 小学 5 年（1）日本語訳

問題英文の日本語訳を確認しよう。

1. この写真を見て。これは，私の犬です。

2. お名前は？　私の名前は，メアリーです。

3. どんなスポーツが好きですか。テニスが好きです。

4. 何色が好きですか。私は青色が好きです。

5. あなたは物語が好きですか。はい，好きです。

6. あなたは定規を持っていますか。いいえ，持っていません。

7. あなたは誕生日に何が欲しいですか。私は赤い帽子が欲しいです。

8. 今日は何曜日ですか。金曜日です。

9. あなたの誕生日はいつですか。私の誕生日は 7 月 4 日です。

10. あなたはどの季節が好きですか。私は夏が好きです。

11. あなたは CD を何枚持っていますか。私は CD を 20 枚持っています。

12. このバッグはいくらですか。500 円です。

13. あなたはこれができますか。いいえ，できません。

14. あなたはどんな科目が好きですか。私は算数が好きです。

15. あなたは何を勉強したいですか。私は理科を勉強したいです。

16. あなたは何になりたいですか。私は歌手になりたいです。

17. どんなカードを持っていますか。私は野球のカードを持っています。

18. あなたは毎日何をしますか。私は毎日公園で遊びます。

19. 彼はマジシャンですか。いいえ，違います。

20. あなたは何時に起きますか。私は 7 時に起きます。

21. 放課後，私は昼ご飯を食べます。その後，友達と遊びます。

22. 彼女は農家です。彼女は歌が上手です。

23. 彼は教師です。彼は野球が上手です。

24. 手を洗ってください。押さないで。

eMET 小学 5 年（1）解答

解答付き英文を見ながら，英語の音声をもう一度聞いてみよう。

1. Look at this photo.　This is my dog.

2. What's (**your**)[1] name?　My name is Mary.

3. What sport do you (**like**)[2]?　I like tennis.

4. What color do you like?　I (**like**)[3] blue.

5. Do you like stories?　Yes, I do.

6. (**Do**)[4] you have a ruler?　No, I don't.

7. What do (**you**)[5] want for your birthday?　I want a red (**cap**)[6].

8. What day is it today?　It's Friday.

9. When is your birthday?　(**My**)[7] birthday is July 4th.

10. What season do you like?　I (**like**)[8] summer.

11. How many CDs do you have?　I have twenty CDs.

12. (**How**)[9] much is this bag?　It's 500 yen.

13. Can you do (**this**)[10]?　No, I can't.

14. What subject do you like?　I (**like**)[11] math.

15. What do you want to study?　I (**want**)[12] to study science.

16. What do you want to be?　(**I**)[13] want to be a singer.

17. What card do (**you**)[14] have?　I have a baseball card.

18. What do (**you**)[15] do every day?　I play in the park every (**day**)[16].

19. Is he a magician?　No, he is not.

20. (**What**)[17] time do you get up?　I get (**up**)[18] at seven.

21. After school I eat lunch.　Then I play with (**my**)[19] friends.

22. She is a farmer.　She can sing well.

23. (**He**)[20] is a teacher.　He is good at baseball.

24. Wash (**your**)[21] hands.　Don't push.

eMET 小学 5 年 (2) 問題

英語の音声を聞きながら，（　　　　）の中に，4 文字以下（最大で 4 文字）の英単語を入れてください。

1. Can you cook well?　Yes, I can.　(　　　　　)^1 can cook curry and rice well.

2. Who is Mary White?　(　　　　　)^2 is my friend.　She is a baker.

3. Where is my (　　　　　)^3?

4. What time do you get up?　I usually (　　　　　)^4 up at five.

5. Are you happy?　Yes, I am.

6. (　　　　　)^5 is my sister.

7. He is Bill.　He can swim (　　　　　)^6.　He can't run fast.

8. Who is this?　This (　　　　　)^7 Kate.

9. Where is the racket?　It's by the desk.

10. Where is your (　　　　　)^8?　You can see it on your left.

11. (　　　　　)^9 can you do?　I can run fast.

12. (　　　　　)^{10} you good at cooking?　No, I'm not.

13. Where is the bookstore?　(　　　　　)^{11} straight for one block.

14. Turn left.　You can see (　　　　　)^{12} on your right.

15. Can you do this?

16. I (　　　　　　)^{13} play the violin.

17. Can she swim?

18. She can (　　　　　　)^{14} the guitar.

19. I want bananas.

20. I eat dinner at six.

21. She (　　　　　　)^{15} sing well.

22. She can't play the guitar.

23. She can skate (　　　　　　)^{16}.

24. Don't go!

eMET 小学 5 年 (2) 問題 日本語訳

問題英文の日本語訳を確認しよう。

1. 料理を上手に作ることができますか。はい，できます。彼はカレーライスを上手に作る
   ことができます。

2. メアリー・ホワイトって，誰ですか。彼女は私の友達です。彼女はパン屋です。

3. 私の本はどこですか。

4. あなたは何時に起きますか。私は普段 5 時に起きます。

5. あなたは幸せですか。はい，幸せです。

6. 彼女は私の妹です。

7. 彼はビルです。彼は速く泳ぐことができます。彼は速く走ることができません。

8. これは誰ですか。これはケイトです。

9. ラケットはどこですか。机のそばです。

10. あなたの本はどこですか。あなたの左側にあります。

11. あなたは何ができますか。私は速く走ることができます。

12. あなたは料理が上手ですか。いいえ，上手じゃありません。

13. 本屋はどこですか。1 ブロック直進してください。

14. 左に曲がってください。そうすると，右側に見えます。

15. あなたはこれができますか。

16. 私はバイオリンを弾くことができます。

17. 彼女は泳げますか。

18. 彼女はギターを弾くことができます。

19. 私はバナナが欲しいです。

20. 私は 6 時に晩ご飯を食べます。

21. 彼女は歌が上手です。

22. 彼女はギターが弾けません。

23. 彼女はスケートが上手です。

24. 行ったらだめです。

eMET 小学 5 年 (2) 解答

解答付き英文を見ながら，英語の音声をもう一度聞いてみよう。

1. Can you cook well?　Yes, I can.　(**He**)^1 can cook curry and rice well.

2. Who is Mary White?　(**She**)^2 is my friend.　She is a baker.

3. Where is my (**book**)^3?

4. What time do you get up?　I usually (**get**)^4 up at five.

5. Are you happy?　Yes, I am.

6. (**She**)^5 is my sister.

7. He is Bill.　He can swim (**fast**)^6.　He can't run fast.

8. Who is this?　This (**is**)^7 Kate.

9. Where is the racket?　It's by the desk.

10. Where is your (**book**)^8?　You can see it on your left.

11. (**What**)^9 can you do?　I can run fast.

12. (**Are**)^{10} you good at cooking?　No, I'm not.

13. Where is the bookstore?　(**Go**)^{11} straight for one block.

14. Turn left.　You can see (**it**)^{12} on your right.

15. Can you do this?

16. I (**can**)^{13} play the violin.

17. Can she swim?

18. She can (**play**)^{14} the guitar.

19. I want bananas.

20. I eat dinner at six.

21. She (**can**)^{15} sing well.

22. She can't play the guitar.

23. She can skate (**well**)^{16}.

24. Don't go!

eMET 小学 5 年 (3) 問題

英語の音声を聞きながら, (　　　) の中に, 4 文字以下 (最大で 4 文字) の英単語を入れてください。

1. What would you like?　I'd like a hamburger.

2. What food (　　　　　)^1 you like?　I like French fries.

3. How much is (　　　　　)^2?　A hamburger is 300 yen.

4. This is an apple.　It's delicious.

5. This is Miss Green.　(　　　　　)^3 is a soccer player.

6. She can run fast.

7. Look (　　　　　)^4 this picture.　This is Mr. Green.

8. Is he good at cooking?　(　　　　　)^5, he is.

9. Is he your hero?　Yes, (　　　　　)^6 is.

10. Is she a junior high school student?　Yes, she (　　　　　)^7.

11. She can dance very well.　That's great!

12. Can he fly (　　　　　)^8 kite?　Yes, he can.

13. Where is the cat?　(　　　　　)^9 is on the box.

14. Where is the fox?　(　　　　　)^{10} is in the box.

15. Where do you want (　　　　　)^{11} go?　I want to go to Italy.

16. Why?　(　　　　　)^{12} want to eat pizza.

17. What do you do （   ）^{13} New Year's Day?   I usually play cards.

18. What do you （   ）^{14} for your birthday?   I want a bicycle.

19. This is （   ）^{15} original menu.

20. I want to go to Boston.

21. I （   ）^{16} to see Susan.

22. Do you help your parents?

23. What （   ）^{17} you like?   I like robots.   I'm in the robot club （   ）^{18} school.

24. Where's the flower shop?   Go straight.   Turn right at the park.

eMET 小学 5 年（3）問題 日本語訳

問題英文の日本語訳を確認しよう。

1. 何にしますか。ハンバーガーにします。

2. あなたはどんな食べ物が好きですか。私はフライドポテトが好きです。

3. それはいくらですか。ハンバーガーは 300 円です。

4. これはリンゴです。おいしいですよ。

5. これはグリーンさんです。彼女はサッカー選手です。

6. 彼女は速く走ることができます。

7. この絵を見て。これはグリーンさんです。

8. 彼は料理が上手ですか。はい。

9. 彼はあなたの憧れですか。はい。

10. 彼女は中学生ですか。はい。

11. 彼女は上手に踊ることができます。それはすばらしい。

12. 彼は凧をあげることができますか。はい，できます。

13. 猫はどこですか。箱の上にいます。

14. キツネはどこですか。箱の中です。

15. あなたはどこに行きたいですか。私はイタリアに行きたいです。

16. なぜですか。ピザが食べたいからです。

17. お正月は何をしますか。私はだいたいトランプをします。

18. 誕生日に何が欲しいですか。自転車が欲しいです。

19. これは私のオリジナルメニューです。

20. 私はボストンに行きたいです。

21. 私はスーザンに会いたいです。

22. あなたは両親の手伝いをしますか。

23. あなたは何が好きですか。私はロボットが好きです。私は学校でロボットクラブに所属しています。

24. 花屋はどこですか。まっすぐ進んでください。公園を右に曲がってください。

eMET 小学 5 年（3）解答

解答付き英文を見ながら，英語の音声をもう一度聞いてみよう。

1. What would you like?　I'd like a hamburger.

2. What food (**do**)^1 you like?　I like French fries.

3. How much is (**it**)^2?　A hamburger is 300 yen.

4. This is an apple.　It's delicious.

5. This is Miss Green.　(**She**)^3 is a soccer player.

6. She can run fast.

7. Look (**at**)^4 this picture.　This is Mr. Green.

8. Is he good at cooking?　(**Yes**)^5, he is.

9. Is he your hero?　Yes, (**he**)^6 is.

10. Is she a junior high school student?　Yes, she (**is**)^7.

11. She can dance very well.　That's great!

12. Can he fly (**a**)^8 kite?　Yes, he can.

13. Where is the cat?　(**It**)^9 is on the box.

14. Where is the fox?　(**It**)^{10} is in the box.

15. Where do you want (**to**)^{11} go?　I want to go to Italy.

16. Why?　(**I**)^{12} want to eat pizza.

17. What do you do (**on**)^{13} New Year's Day?　I usually play cards.

18. What do you (**want**)^{14} for your birthday?　I want a bicycle.

19. This is (**my**)^{15} original menu.

20. I want to go to Boston.

21. I (**want**)^{16} to see Susan.

22. Do you help your parents?

23. What (**do**)^{17} you like?　I like robots.　I'm in the robot club (**at**)^{18} school.

24. Where's the flower shop?　Go straight.　Turn right at the park.

eMET 小学 5 年（4）問題

英語の音声を聞きながら，（　　　　　）の中に，4 文字以下（最大で 4 文字）の英単語を入れてください。

1. My name is Kate.　I like singing.

2. My hero （　　　　　）[1] my English teacher.　He can sing very well.

3. He （　　　　　）[2] a very good teacher.

4. Who is your hero?　（　　　　　）[3] hero is my brother.

5. Why is he your （　　　　　）[4]?　He is good at cooking.

6. He is always kind （　　　　　）[5] me.

7. Are you good at playing soccer?　Yes, I （　　　　　）[6].

8. What would you like?　I'd like spaghetti.

9. How much is （　　　　　）[7] spaghetti?　It's 500 yen.

10. Where do you want to go?　I want （　　　　　）[8] go to the amusement park.

11. I want to （　　　　　）[9] to the beach.

12. Where is the station?　Go straight.　Turn right at （　　　　　）[10] second corner.

13. You can see it on your right.

14. This （　　　　　）[11] Miss Davis.　She can swim very fast.　She is （　　　　）[12].　She is my favorite swimmer.

15. Where do you want to (   )[13]?   I want to go to Africa.

16. This is Mr. Brown.   He (   )[14] a firefighter.

17. Who is your best friend?   My best friend (   )[15] Kate.

18. She is a police officer.

19. What do you want (   )[16] lunch?   I want a hot dog.

20. What would you (   )[17]?   I'd like pizza.

21. What is this city famous for?   It's famous for its (   )[18] festival.

22. What is the town famous for?   It's famous for its beef.

23. What (   )[19] your city famous for?   My city is famous for (   )[20] castle.

24. I want to see a rocket.

eMET 小学 5 年（4）問題 日本語訳

問題英文の日本語訳を確認しよう。

1. 私の名前はケイトです。私は歌うことが好きです。

2. 私の憧れの人は，私の英語の先生です。彼は歌がとても上手です。

3. 彼はとても良い先生です。

4. 憧れの人は誰ですか。兄です。

5. なぜ彼はあなたの憧れですか。料理が上手だからです。

6. 彼はいつも私に親切です。

7. あなたはサッカーが得意ですか。はい，得意です。

8. 何にしますか。スパゲッティにします。

9. スパゲッティはいくらしますか。500 円です。

10. どこに行きたいですか。私は遊園地に行きたいです。

11. 私は海に行きたいです。

12. 駅はどこですか。まっすぐ進んでください。2 つ目の角を右に曲がってください。

13. あなたの右側にそれが見えます。

14. これはデイビスさんです。彼女はとても速く泳ぐことができます。彼女はかっこいいです。彼女は私のお気に入りの水泳選手です。

15. あなたはどこに行きたいですか。私はアフリカに行きたいです。

16. これはブラウンさんです。彼は消防士です。

17. あなたの一番の友達は誰ですか。私の一番の友達はケイトです。

18. 彼女は警官です。

19. あなたは昼に何が食べたいですか。私はホットドッグが食べたいです。

20. 何にしますか。ピザにします。

21. この都市は何で有名ですか。雪祭りで有名です。

22. その町は何で有名ですか。牛肉で有名です。

23. あなたの市は何で有名ですか。私の市は城で有名です。

24. 私はロケットが見たいです。

eMET 小学 5 年 (4) 解答

解答付き英文を見ながら，英語の音声をもう一度聞いてみよう。

1. My name is Kate.　I like singing.

2. My hero (**is**)[1] my English teacher.　He can sing very well.

3. He (**is**)[2] a very good teacher.

4. Who is your hero?　(**My**)[3] hero is my brother.

5. Why is he your (**hero**)[4]?　He is good at cooking.

6. He is always kind (**to**)[5] me.

7. Are you good at playing soccer?　Yes, I (**am**)[6].

8. What would you like?　I'd like spaghetti.

9. How much is (**the**)[7] spaghetti?　It's 500 yen.

10. Where do you want to go?　I want (**to**)[8] go to the amusement park.

11. I want to (**go**)[9] to the beach.

12. Where is the station?　Go straight.　Turn right at (**the**)[10] second corner.

13. You can see it on your right.

14. This (**is**)[11] Miss Davis.　She can swim very fast.　She is (**cool**)[12].　She is my favorite swimmer.

15. Where do you want to (**go**)[13]?　I want to go to Africa.

16. This is Mr. Brown.　He (**is**)[14] a firefighter.

17. Who is your best friend?　My best friend (**is**)[15] Kate.

18. She is a police officer.

19. What do you want (**for**)[16] lunch?　I want a hot dog.

20. What would you (**like**)[17]?　I'd like pizza.

21. What is this city famous for?　It's famous for its (**snow**)[18] festival.

22. What is the town famous for?　It's famous for its beef.

23. What (**is**)[19] your city famous for?　My city is famous for (**its**)[20] castle.

24. I want to see a rocket.

eMET 小学 **6** 年 (**1**) 問題

英語の音声を聞きながら, (　　　　　　) の中に, 4 文字以下 (最大で 4 文字) の英単語を入れてください。

1. I'm Emily.　I'm from Spain.

2. Where are you from?

3. What animals do you (　　　　　　)^1?　I like dogs.

4. When is your birthday?　My birthday (　　　　　　)^2 May 4th.

5. I can play the recorder well.　That's great!

6. My (　　　　　　)^3 is John.　I'm from Canada.

7. I like music.　I can play (　　　　　　)^4 piano.

8. My favorite place is the music room.

9. I'm good at painting pictures.

10. Is there anything (　　　　　　)^5 we can do for you?

11. What's your favorite sport?　My favorite sport (　　　　　　)^6 baseball.

12. Where do you live?　I live in France.

13. I'm from London.

14. I'm (　　　　　　)^7 at singing.

15. What fruit do you like?　I like oranges.

16. (　　　　　　)^8 vegetable do you like?　I like tomatoes.

17. Welcome to my （　　　　　　）^{9}.

18. My town is beautiful.　We have a big （　　　　　　）^{10}.

19. We can enjoy fishing.

20. In summer, we have a summer festival.　You （　　　　　　）^{11} enjoy delicious food.　You can enjoy dancing, too.

21. We have an entrance ceremony （　　　　　　）^{12} April.　We don't have an entrance ceremony in September.

22. We have the Star Festival （　　　　　　）^{13} July.

23. You can visit the temple today.　It's beautiful.

24. You can see （　　　　　　）^{14} festival in August.　It's very interesting.

eMET 小学 6 年（1）問題 日本語訳

問題英文の日本語訳を確認しよう。

1. 私はエミリーです。私はスペイン出身です。

2. あなたの出身地はどこですか。

3. どんな動物が好きですか。私は犬が好きです。

4. あなたの誕生日はいつですか。私の誕生日は 5 月 4 日です。

5. 私はリコーダーを上手に演奏できます。すばらしいですね。

6. 私の名前はジョンです。私はカナダ出身です。

7. 私は音楽が好きです。私はピアノを弾くことができます。

8. 私のお気に入りの場所は音楽室です。

9. 私は絵を描くことが得意です。

10. あなたのために何かできることはありますか。

11. あなたのお気に入りのスポーツは何ですか。私のお気に入りのスポーツは野球です。

12. どこに住んでいますか。私はフランスに住んでいます。

13. 私はロンドン出身です。

14. 私は歌うことが得意です。

15. あなたはどんな果物が好きですか。私はオレンジが好きです。

16. あなたはどんな野菜が好きですか。私はトマトが好きです。

17. 私の町へようこそ。

18. 私の町は美しいです。大きい公園があります。

19. 私たちは釣りを楽しむことができます。

20. 夏には，夏祭りがあります。おいしい食べ物を食べることができます。踊りを楽しむこともできます。

21. 私たちは 4 月に入学式があります。9 月には入学式がありません。

22. 7 月に七夕祭りがあります。

23. 今日そのお寺を訪れることができます。美しいですよ。

24. 8 月にその祭りを見ることができます。とても面白いですよ。

eMET 小学 6 年（1）解答

解答付き英文を見ながら，英語の音声をもう一度聞いてみよう。

1. I'm Emily.　I'm from Spain.

2. Where are you from?

3. What animals do you（ **like** ）^{1}?　I like dogs.

4. When is your birthday?　My birthday（ **is** ）^{2} May 4th.

5. I can play the recorder well.　That's great!

6. My（ **name** ）^{3} is John.　I'm from Canada.

7. I like music.　I can play（ **the** ）^{4} piano.

8. My favorite place is the music room.

9. I'm good at painting pictures.

10. Is there anything（ **that** ）^{5} we can do for you?

11. What's your favorite sport?　My favorite sport（ **is** ）^{6} baseball.

12. Where do you live?　I live in France.

13. I'm from London.

14. I'm（ **good** ）^{7} at singing.

15. What fruit do you like?　I like oranges.

16. （ **What** ）^{8} vegetable do you like?　I like tomatoes.

17. Welcome to my（ **town** ）^{9}.

18. My town is beautiful.　We have a big（ **park** ）^{10}.

19. We can enjoy fishing.

20. In summer, we have a summer festival.　You（ **can** ）^{11} enjoy delicious food.　You can enjoy dancing, too.

21. We have an entrance ceremony（ **in** ）^{12} April.　We don't have an entrance ceremony in September.

22. We have the Star Festival（ **in** ）^{13} July.

23. You can visit the temple today.　It's beautiful.

24. You can see（ **the** ）^{14} festival in August.　It's very interesting.

eMET 小学 **6** 年 (2) 問題

英語の音声を聞きながら, (　　　　) の中に, 4 文字以下 (最大で 4 文字) の英単語を入れてください。

1. Let's go to India.　India is a nice country.

2. Why do (　　　　　)^1 like India?

3. Are you from Mexico?　No, I'm not.

4. Where do (　　　　　)^2 want to go?　I want to go (　　　　　　)^3 Canada.

5. You can enjoy the flowers in May.

6. You can (　　　　　)^4 lunch under the trees.

7. Can I go?　No, you can't.

8. Let's watch volleyball together.

9. I (　　　　　)^5 to watch table tennis.　It's exciting.

10. This is our town.　We have (　　　　　)^6 nice library.　We have a zoo.

11. What do (　　　　　)^7 want in our town?　I want a museum.

12. I'm Michael.　I'm (　　　　　)^8 Australia.

13. I like Japanese food.　I like reading Japanese books.

14. Where did you (　　　　　)^9 this summer?　I went to the beach.

15. How was (　　　　　　)^{10} summer vacation?　It was great.　I enjoyed camping.

16. You can climb the mountain.　It's very beautiful.　Please (　　　　　)^{11} it.

17. Are you a giraffe?　Yes, I am.

18. (　　　　　　)^{12} can play with the elephants.

19. You can buy good (　　　　　)^{13}.

20. You can visit the city by boat.

21. Let's sing (　　　　　)^{14} song.

22. Let's cut the cake.

23. I am tall.

24. (　　　　　)^{15} have long legs.

eMET 小学 6 年（2）問題 日本語訳

問題英文の日本語訳を確認しよう。

1. インドに行きましょう。インドはすばらしい国です。

2. なぜインドが好きなんですか。

3. あなたはメキシコ出身ですか。いいえ，違います。

4. あなたはどこに行きたいですか。私はカナダに行きたいです。

5. 5月に花を楽しむことができます。

6. 木の下でお昼を食べることができます。

7. 私は行けますか。いいえ，行けません。

8. 一緒にバレーボールを見ましょう。

9. 私は卓球が見たいです。わくわくさせてくれますよね。

10. これは私たちの町です。すばらしい図書館があります。動物園があります。

11. 私たちの町に何が欲しいですか。私は博物館が欲しいです。

12. 私はマイケルです。私はオーストラリア出身です。

13. 私は日本食が好きです。私は日本の本を読むことが好きです。

14. この夏，あなたはどこに行きましたか。私は海に行きました。

15. 夏休みはどうでしたか。よかったですよ。キャンプを楽しみました。

16. その山に登ることができます。とても美しいですよ。試してみてください。

17. あなたはキリンですか。はい，そうです。

18. 象と遊ぶことができます。

19. いいお茶が買えますよ。

20. あなたは船でその都市を訪れることができます。

21. 歌を歌いましょう。

22. ケーキを切りましょう。

23. 私は背が高いです。

24. 私は足が長いです。

eMET 小学 **6** 年 (2) 解答

解答付き英文を見ながら，英語の音声をもう一度聞いてみよう。

1. Let's go to India.　India is a nice country.

2. Why do (**you**)[1] like India?

3. Are you from Mexico?　No, I'm not.

4. Where do (**you**)[2] want to go?　I want to go (**to**)[3] Canada.

5. You can enjoy the flowers in May.

6. You can (**eat**)[4] lunch under the trees.

7. Can I go?　No, you can't.

8. Let's watch volleyball together.

9. I (**want**)[5] to watch table tennis.　It's exciting.

10. This is our town.　We have (**a**)[6] nice library.　We have a zoo.

11. What do (**you**)[7] want in our town?　I want a museum.

12. I'm Michael.　I'm (**from**)[8] Australia.

13. I like Japanese food.　I like reading Japanese books.

14. Where did you (**go**)[9] this summer?　I went to the beach.

15. How was (**your**)[10] summer vacation?　It was great.　I enjoyed camping.

16. You can climb the mountain.　It's very beautiful.　Please (**try**)[11] it.

17. Are you a giraffe?　Yes, I am.

18. (**You**)[12] can play with the elephants.

19. You can buy good (**tea**)[13].

20. You can visit the city by boat.

21. Let's sing (**a**)[14] song.

22. Let's cut the cake.

23. I am tall.

24. (**I**)[15] have long legs.

eMET 小学 6 年（3）問題

英語の音声を聞きながら, （　　　　）の中に, 4 文字以下（最大で 4 文字）の英単語を入れてください。

1. Where do dolphins live?   They live in the sea.

2. Where (　　　　)^1 lions live?   They live in the savanna.

3. We can (　　　　)^2 English books in the library.

4. We can play baseball at (　　　　)^3 park.

5. In London, we can ride on a (　　　　)^4 on the river.   We can see castles, too.

6. We (　　　　)^5 in Florida.   We have beautiful beaches.   We can swim in (　　　　)^6 clear water.   We love Florida very much.

7. What country do you (　　　　)^7 to visit?   I want to visit France.

8. Why?   I want (　　　　)^8 see the castle.

9. You can eat French bread.   It's delicious.

10. He is (　　　　)^9 athlete.

11. He is from Brazil.   He can play tennis very (　　　　)^{10}.   He is famous.

12. What did you do yesterday?   I played tennis yesterday.

13. (　　　　)^{11} did you do last weekend?   I played soccer last Sunday. It (　　　　)^{12} exciting.

14. Are you hungry?   I usually eat beef curry at home.

15. Where (   )^{13} the beef from?   It is from Australia.

16. Where do (   )^{14} want to go?   I want to go (   )^{15} the bank.

17. Go straight.   Turn right at the first corner.

18. What (   )^{16} you want to be?   I want to (   )^{17} a carpenter.

19. I want to build a house.

20. What is (   )^{18} best memory?   My best memory is the school trip.

21. We (   )^{19} to China in January.

22. What did you see?   We (   )^{20} a lot of temples.

23. I want to see (   )^{21} singer.

24. I want to go to the zoo.

eMET 小学 6 年（3）問題 日本語訳

問題英文の日本語訳を確認しよう。

1. イルカはどこに住んでいますか。海に住んでいます。

2. ライオンはどこに住んでいますか。サバンナに住んでいます。

3. 私たちは図書館で英語の本を読むことができます。

4. 私たちは公園で野球をすることができます。

5. ロンドンでは，川で船に乗ることができます。城も見ることができます。

6. 私たちはフロリダに住んでいます。きれいな浜辺があります。澄んだ水の中を泳ぐことができます。私たちはフロリダが大好きです。

7. あなたはどの国を訪れたいですか。私はフランスを訪れたいです。

8. なぜですか。城が見たいからです。

9. フランスパンを食べることができます。とてもおいしいですよ。

10. 彼はアスリートです。

11. 彼はブラジル出身です。彼はとても上手にテニスをすることができます。彼は有名です。

12. 昨日何をしましたか。私は昨日テニスをしました。

13. 先週末は何をしましたか。私は先週の日曜日にサッカーをしました。とても楽しかったです。

14. 腹ペコですか。私は普段家でビーフカレーを食べます。

15. そのビーフはどこから来ていますか。オーストラリアです。

16. あなたはどこに行きたいですか。銀行に行きたいです。

17. まっすぐ進んでください。最初の角を右に曲がってください。

18. あなたは何になりたいですか。私は大工になりたいです。

19. 私は家を建てたいです。

20. あなたの一番の思い出は何ですか。私の一番の思い出は修学旅行です。

21. 私たちは 1 月に中国に行きました。

22. 何を見ましたか。お寺をたくさん見ました。

23. 私はその歌手を見たいです。

24. 私は動物園に行きたいです。

eMET 小学 6 年（3）解答

解答付き英文を見ながら，英語の音声をもう一度聞いてみよう。

1. Where do dolphins live?　They live in the sea.

2. Where (**do**)[1] lions live?　They live in the savanna.

3. We can (**read**)[2] English books in the library.

4. We can play baseball at (**the**)[3] park.

5. In London, we can ride on a (**boat**)[4] on the river.　We can see castles, too.

6. We (**live**)[5] in Florida.　We have beautiful beaches.　We can swim in (**the**)[6] clear water.　We love Florida very much.

7. What country do you (**want**)[7] to visit?　I want to visit France.

8. Why?　I want (**to**)[8] see the castle.

9. You can eat French bread.　It's delicious.

10. He is (**an**)[9] athlete.

11. He is from Brazil.　He can play tennis very (**well**)[10].　He is famous.

12. What did you do yesterday?　I played tennis yesterday.

13. (**What**)[11] did you do last weekend?　I played soccer last Sunday.　It (**was**)[12] exciting.

14. Are you hungry?　I usually eat beef curry at home.

15. Where (**is**)[13] the beef from?　It is from Australia.

16. Where do (**you**)[14] want to go?　I want to go (**to**)[15] the bank.

17. Go straight.　Turn right at the first corner.

18. What (**do**)[16] you want to be?　I want to (**be**)[17] a carpenter.

19. I want to build a house.

20. What is (**your**)[18] best memory?　My best memory is the school trip.

21. We (**went**)[19] to China in January.

22. What did you see?　We (**saw**)[20] a lot of temples.

23. I want to see (**the**)[21] singer.

24. I want to go to the zoo.

eMET 小学 6 年 (4) 問題

英語の音声を聞きながら, (　　　　) の中に, 4 文字以下 (最大で 4 文字) の英単語を入れてください。

1. What club do you want to join?　(　　　　　)^1 want to join the volleyball club.

2. What school event do (　　　　)^2 want to enjoy?　I want to enjoy sports day.

3. What (　　　　)^3 you want to be?　I want to (　　　　)^4 a teacher.

4. Who is your favorite sports player?　My favorite sports player is Michael Jordan.

5. He (　　　　)^5 a good basketball player.

6. I'm Fred.　I want to be a scientist.

7. (　　　　)^6?　I like my science classes.

8. My name is Mary White.　I (　　　　)^7 a lot of taxis in New York.

9. My favorite memory is the summer (　　　　)^8.

10. I went to the zoo.　I saw pandas.

11. (　　　　)^9 enjoyed taking pictures.

12. I ate a hamburger.

13. Who is this?　He (　　　　)^{10} Bill, a famous artist.

14. He can sing and dance very well.

15. (   )^{11} is this?   This is Kate.   She is from Korea.

16. (   )^{12} do you want to enjoy?   I want to enjoy (   )^{13} chorus contest.

17. What club do you want to join?   (   )^{14} like music.

18. I can play the drums.   I want to (   )^{15} the brass band.

19. What club do you want (   )^{16} join?   I want to join the science club.   (   )^{17}, too.

20. What do you want to be?   (   )^{18} want to be a soccer player.

21. I like soccer.

22. What (   )^{19} do you want to join?   I want (   )^{20} join the cooking club.

23. What subject do you want (   )^{21} study hard?   I want to study math hard.

24. We (   )^{22} many events and activities in junior high school life.

eMET 小学 6 年（4）問題 日本語訳

問題英文の日本語訳を確認しよう。

1. あなたはどのクラブに入りたいですか。私はバレーボールクラブに入りたいです。

2. あなたはどんな学校行事を楽しみたいですか。体育祭を楽しみたいです。

3. あなたは何になりたいですか。先生になりたいです。

4. あなたのお気に入りのスポーツ選手は誰ですか。私のお気に入りのスポーツ選手は，マイケル・ジョーダンです。

5. 彼はすばらしいバスケットボール選手です。

6. 私はフレッドです。私は科学者になりたいです。

7. なぜですか。理科の授業が好きだからです。

8. 私の名前はメアリー・ホワイトです。私はニューヨークでタクシーをたくさん見ました。

9. 私のお気に入りの思い出は夏のキャンプです。

10. 私は動物園に行きました。私はパンダを見ました。

11. 私は写真を撮って楽しみました。

12. 私はハンバーガーを食べました。

13. これは誰ですか。彼はビルで，有名なアーティストです。

14. 彼はとても上手に歌って踊れます。

15. これは誰ですか。これはケイトです。彼女は韓国出身です。

16. あなたは何を楽しみたいですか。合唱コンクールを楽しみたいです。

17. あなたはどのクラブに入りたいですか。私は音楽が好きです。

18. 私はドラムを演奏することができます。私は吹奏楽部に入りたいです。

19. あなたは何クラブに入りたいですか。私は理科クラブに入りたいです。私もです。

20. あなたは何になりたいですか。私はサッカー選手になりたいです。

21. 私はサッカーが好きです。

22. あなたはどんなクラブに入りたいですか。私は料理クラブに入りたいです。

23. あなたはどんな科目を一所懸命勉強したいですか。私は算数を一所懸命勉強したいです。

24. 中学校生活にはたくさんの行事と活動があります。

eMET 小学 6 年 (4) 解答

解答付き英文を見ながら，英語の音声をもう一度聞いてみよう。

1. What club do you want to join?　(**I**)^1 want to join the volleyball club.

2. What school event do (**you**)^2 want to enjoy?　I want to enjoy sports day.

3. What (**do**)^3 you want to be?　I want to (**be**)^4 a teacher.

4. Who is your favorite sports player?　My favorite sports player is Michael Jordan.

5. He (**is**)^5 a good basketball player.

6. I'm Fred.　I want to be a scientist.

7. (**Why**)^6?　I like my science classes.

8. My name is Mary White.　I (**saw**)^7 a lot of taxis in New York.

9. My favorite memory is the summer (**camp**)^8.

10. I went to the zoo.　I saw pandas.

11. (**I**)^9 enjoyed taking pictures.

12. I ate a hamburger.

13. Who is this?　He (**is**)^{10} Bill, a famous artist.

14. He can sing and dance very well.

15. (**Who**)^{11} is this?　This is Kate.　She is from Korea.

16. (**What**)^{12} do you want to enjoy?　I want to enjoy (**the**)^{13} chorus contest.

17. What club do you want to join?　(**I**)^{14} like music.

18. I can play the drums.　I want to (**join**)^{15} the brass band.

19. What club do you want (**to**)^{16} join?　I want to join the science club.　(**Me**)^{17}, too.

20. What do you want to be?　(**I**)^{18} want to be a soccer player.

21. I like soccer.

22. What (**club**)^{19} do you want to join?　I want (**to**)^{20} join the cooking club.

23. What subject do you want (**to**)^{21} study hard?　I want to study math hard.

24. We (**have**)^{22} many events and activities in junior high school life.

eMET 小学 5 年・6 年総合（1）問題

英語の音声を聞きながら,（ ）の中に,4 文字以下（最大で 4 文字）の英単語を入れてください。

1. Look at this photo.　This is my dog.

2. What's （　　　　　　）^{1} name?　My name is Mary.

3. What sport do you （　　　　　　）^{2}?　I like tennis.

4. What time do you get （　　　　　　）^{3}?　I usually get up at five.

5. Are you happy?　（　　　　　　）^{4}, I am.

6. She is my sister.

7. Look at （　　　　　　）^{5} picture.　This is Mr. Green.

8. Is he good at cooking?　Yes, （　　　　　　）^{6} is.

9. Is he your hero?　Yes, he （　　　　　　）^{7}.

10. Where do you want to go?　I want （　　　　　　）^{8} go to the amusement park.

11. I want to （　　　　　　）^{9} to the beach.

12. Where is the station?　Go straight.　Turn right at （　　　　　　）^{10} second corner.

13. I'm from London.

14. I'm good at singing.

15. What fruit do (   )^{11} like? I like oranges.

16. You can climb the mountain. It's very beautiful. Please (   )^{12} it.

17. Are you a giraffe? Yes, I am.

18. (   )^{13} can play with the elephants.

19. I want to build a house.

20. (   )^{14} is your best memory? My best memory is the school (   )^{15}.

21. We went to China in January.

22. What club do (   )^{16} want to join? I want to join (   )^{17} cooking club.

23. What subject do you want to study hard? (   )^{18} want to study math hard.

24. We have many events (   )^{19} activities in junior high school life.

eMET 小学 5 年・6 年総合 (1) 問題 日本語訳

問題英文の日本語訳を確認しよう。

1. この写真を見て。これは，私の犬です。

2. お名前は？ 私の名前は，メアリーです。

3. どんなスポーツが好きですか。テニスが好きです。

4. あなたは何時に起きますか。私は普段 5 時に起きます。

5. あなたは幸せですか。はい，幸せです。

6. 彼女は私の妹です。

7. この絵を見て。これはグリーンさんです。

8. 彼は料理が上手ですか。はい。

9. 彼はあなたの憧れですか。はい。

10. どこに行きたいですか。私は遊園地に行きたいです。

11. 私は海に行きたいです。

12. 駅はどこですか。まっすぐ進んでください。2 つ目の角を右に曲がってください。

13. 私はロンドン出身です。

14. 私は歌うことが得意です。

15. あなたはどんな果物が好きですか。私はオレンジが好きです。

16. その山に登ることができます。とても美しいですよ。試してみてください。

17. あなたはキリンですか。はい，そうです。

18. 象と遊ぶことができます。

19. 私は家を建てたいです。

20. あなたの一番の思い出は何ですか。私の一番の思い出は修学旅行です。

21. 私たちは 1 月に中国に行きました。

22. あなたはどんなクラブに入りたいですか。私は料理クラブに入りたいです。

23. あなたはどんな科目を一所懸命勉強したいですか。私は算数を一所懸命勉強したいです。

24. 中学校生活にはたくさんの行事と活動があります。

eMET 小学 5 年・6 年総合（1）解答

解答付き英文を見ながら，英語の音声をもう一度聞いてみよう。

1. Look at this photo.　This is my dog.

2. What's (**your**)[1] name?　My name is Mary.

3. What sport do you (**like**)[2]?　I like tennis.

4. What time do you get (**up**)[3]?　I usually get up at five.

5. Are you happy?　(**Yes**)[4], I am.

6. She is my sister.

7. Look at (**this**)[5] picture.　This is Mr. Green.

8. Is he good at cooking?　Yes, (**he**)[6] is.

9. Is he your hero?　Yes, he (**is**)[7].

10. Where do you want to go?　I want (**to**)[8] go to the amusement park.

11. I want to (**go**)[9] to the beach.

12. Where is the station?　Go straight.　Turn right at (**the**)[10] second corner.

13. I'm from London.

14. I'm good at singing.

15. What fruit do (**you**)[11] like?　I like oranges.

16. You can climb the mountain.　It's very beautiful.　Please (**try**)[12] it.

17. Are you a giraffe?　Yes, I am.

18. (**You**)[13] can play with the elephants.

19. I want to build a house.

20. (**What**)[14] is your best memory?　My best memory is the school (**trip**)[15].

21. We went to China in January.

22. What club do (**you**)[16] want to join?　I want to join (**the**)[17] cooking club.

23. What subject do you want to study hard?　(**I**)[18] want to study math hard.

24. We have many events (**and**)[19] activities in junior high school life.

eMET 小学 5 年・6 年総合 (2) 問題

英語の音声を聞きながら, (   ) の中に, 4 文字以下 (最大で 4 文字) の英単語を入れてください。

1. What color do you like?   I like blue.

2. (   )[1] you like stories?   Yes, I do.

3. Do you (   )[2] a ruler?   No, I don't.

4. He is Bill.   He (   )[3] swim fast.   He can't run fast.

5. Who (   )[4] this?   This is Kate.

6. Where is the racket?   It's by (   )[5] desk.

7. Is she a junior high school student?   Yes, she (   )[6].

8. She can dance very well.   That's great!

9. Can he fly (   )[7] kite?   Yes, he can.

10. You can see (   )[8] on your right.

11. This is Miss Davis.   She can swim (   )[9] fast.   She is cool.
    She is my favorite swimmer.

12. Where (   )[10] you want to go?   I want to (   )[11] to
    Africa.

13. What vegetable do you like?   I like tomatoes.

14. Welcome (   )[12] my town.

15. My town is beautiful. We have ( )^{13} big park.

16. You can buy good tea.

17. ( )^{14} can visit the city by boat.

18. Let's sing ( )^{15} song.

19. What did you see? We saw ( )^{16} lot of temples.

20. I want to see the singer.

21. ( )^{17} want to go to the zoo.

22. What ( )^{18} do you want to join? I want ( )^{19} join the volleyball club.

23. What school event do you want ( )^{20} enjoy? I want to enjoy sports day.

24. What do you ( )^{21} to be? I want to be a teacher.

eMET 小学 5 年・6 年総合（2）問題 日本語訳

問題英文の日本語訳を確認しよう。

1. 何色が好きですか。私は青色が好きです。

2. あなたは物語が好きですか。はい，好きです。

3. あなたは定規を持っていますか。いいえ，持っていません。

4. 彼はビルです。彼は速く泳ぐことができます。彼は速く走ることができません。

5. これは誰ですか。これはケイトです。

6. ラケットはどこですか。机のそばです。

7. 彼女は中学生ですか。はい。

8. 彼女は上手に踊ることができます。それはすばらしい。

9. 彼は凧をあげることができますか。はい，できます。

10. あなたの右側にそれが見えます。

11. これはデイビスさんです。彼女はとても速く泳ぐことができます。彼女はかっこいいです。彼女は私のお気に入りの水泳選手です。

12. あなたはどこに行きたいですか。私はアフリカに行きたいです。

13. あなたはどんな野菜が好きですか。私はトマトが好きです。

14. 私の町へようこそ。

15. 私の町は美しいです。大きい公園があります。

16. いいお茶が買えますよ。

17. あなたは船でその都市を訪れることができます。

18. 歌を歌いましょう。

19. 何を見ましたか。お寺をたくさん見ました。

20. 私はその歌手を見たいです。

21. 私は動物園に行きたいです。

22. あなたはどのクラブに入りたいですか。私はバレーボールクラブに入りたいです。

23. あなたはどんな学校行事を楽しみたいですか。体育祭を楽しみたいです。

24. あなたは何になりたいですか。先生になりたいです。

eMET 小学 5 年・6 年総合 (2) 解答

解答付き英文を見ながら，英語の音声をもう一度聞いてみよう。

1. What color do you like?   I like blue.

2. (**Do**)[1] you like stories?   Yes, I do.

3. Do you (**have**)[2] a ruler?   No, I don't.

4. He is Bill.   He (**can**)[3] swim fast.   He can't run fast.

5. Who (**is**)[4] this?   This is Kate.

6. Where is the racket?   It's by (**the**)[5] desk.

7. Is she a junior high school student?   Yes, she (**is**)[6].

8. She can dance very well.   That's great!

9. Can he fly (**a**)[7] kite?   Yes, he can.

10. You can see (**it**)[8] on your right.

11. This is Miss Davis.   She can swim (**very**)[9] fast.   She is cool.   She is my favorite swimmer.

12. Where (**do**)[10] you want to go?   I want to (**go**)[11] to Africa.

13. What vegetable do you like?   I like tomatoes.

14. Welcome (**to**)[12] my town.

15. My town is beautiful.   We have (**a**)[13] big park.

16. You can buy good tea.

17. (**You**)[14] can visit the city by boat.

18. Let's sing (**a**)[15] song.

19. What did you see?   We saw (**a**)[16] lot of temples.

20. I want to see the singer.

21. (**I**)[17] want to go to the zoo.

22. What (**club**)[18] do you want to join?   I want (**to**)[19] join the volleyball club.

23. What school event do you want (**to**)[20] enjoy?   I want to enjoy sports day.

24. What do you (**want**)[21] to be?   I want to be a teacher.

eMET 小学 5 年・6 年総合 (3) 問題

英語の音声を聞きながら，(　　　　　) の中に，4 文字以下 (最大で 4 文字) の英単語を入れてください。

1. What do you want for your birthday?　I (　　　　　)[1] a red cap.

2. What day is it today?　It's Friday.

3. (　　　　　)[2] is your birthday?　My birthday is July 4th.

4. Where is (　　　　　)[3] book?　You can see it on your (　　　　　)[4].

5. What can you do?　I can run (　　　　　)[5].

6. Are you good at cooking?　No, I'm not.

7. Where (　　　　　)[6] the cat?　It is on the box.

8. Where (　　　　　)[7] the fox?　It is in the box.

9. Where (　　　　　)[8] you want to go?　I want to (　　　　　)[9] to Italy.

10. This is Mr. Brown.　He is a firefighter.

11. Who (　　　　　)[10] your best friend?　My best friend is Kate.

12. She is (　　　　　)[11] police officer.

13. We can enjoy fishing.

14. In summer, we have a summer festival.　You (　　　　　)[12] enjoy delicious food.　You can enjoy dancing, too.

15. We have an entrance ceremony (   )^{13} April.　We don't have an entrance ceremony in September.

16. Let's cut (   )^{14} cake.

17. I am tall.

18. I have long (   )^{15}.

19. Where do dolphins live?　They live in the sea.

20. Where (   )^{16} lions live?　They live in the savanna.

21. We can (   )^{17} English books in the library.

22. Who is your favorite sports player?　My favorite sports player is Michael Jordan.

23. (   )^{18} is a good basketball player.

24. I'm Fred.　I want to (   )^{19} a scientist.

eMET 小学 5 年・6 年総合（3）問題 日本語訳

問題英文の日本語訳を確認しよう。

1. あなたは誕生日に何が欲しいですか。私は赤い帽子が欲しいです。

2. 今日は何曜日ですか。金曜日です。

3. あなたの誕生日はいつですか。私の誕生日は 7 月 4 日です。

4. あなたの本はどこですか。あなたの左側にあります。

5. あなたは何ができますか。私は速く走ることができます。

6. あなたは料理が上手ですか。いいえ，上手じゃありません。

7. 猫はどこですか。箱の上にいます。

8. キツネはどこですか。箱の中です。

9. あなたはどこに行きたいですか。私はイタリアに行きたいです。

10. これはブラウンさんです。彼は消防士です。

11. あなたの一番の友達は誰ですか。私の一番の友達はケイトです。

12. 彼女は警官です。

13. 私たちは釣りを楽しむことができます。

14. 夏には，夏祭りがあります。おいしい食べ物を食べることができます。踊りを楽しむこともできます。

15. 私たちは 4 月に入学式があります。9 月には入学式がありません。

16. ケーキを切りましょう。

17. 私は背が高いです。

18. 私は足が長いです。

19. イルカはどこに住んでいますか。海に住んでいます。

20. ライオンはどこに住んでいますか。サバンナに住んでいます。

21. 私たちは図書館で英語の本を読むことができます。

22. あなたのお気に入りのスポーツ選手は誰ですか。私のお気に入りのスポーツ選手は，マイケル・ジョーダンです。

23. 彼はすばらしいバスケットボール選手です。

24. 私はフレッドです。私は科学者になりたいです。

eMET 小学 5 年・6 年総合 (3) 解答

解答付き英文を見ながら，英語の音声をもう一度聞いてみよう。

1. What do you want for your birthday?　I (**want**)[1] a red cap.

2. What day is it today?　It's Friday.

3. (**When**)[2] is your birthday?　My birthday is July 4th.

4. Where is (**your**)[3] book?　You can see it on your (**left**)[4].

5. What can you do?　I can run (**fast**)[5].

6. Are you good at cooking?　No, I'm not.

7. Where (**is**)[6] the cat?　It is on the box.

8. Where (**is**)[7] the fox?　It is in the box.

9. Where (**do**)[8] you want to go?　I want to (**go**)[9] to Italy.

10. This is Mr. Brown.　He is a firefighter.

11. Who (**is**)[10] your best friend?　My best friend is Kate.

12. She is (**a**)[11] police officer.

13. We can enjoy fishing.

14. In summer, we have a summer festival.　You (**can**)[12] enjoy delicious food.　You can enjoy dancing, too.

15. We have an entrance ceremony (**in**)[13] April.　We don't have an entrance ceremony in September.

16. Let's cut (**the**)[14] cake.

17. I am tall.

18. I have long (**legs**)[15].

19. Where do dolphins live?　They live in the sea.

20. Where (**do**)[16] lions live?　They live in the savanna.

21. We can (**read**)[17] English books in the library.

22. Who is your favorite sports player?　My favorite sports player is Michael Jordan.

23. (**He**)[18] is a good basketball player.

24. I'm Fred.　I want to (**be**)[19] a scientist.

eMET 小学 5 年・6 年総合 (4) 問題

英語の音声を聞きながら, (　　　　　) の中に, 4 文字以下 (最大で 4 文字) の英単語を入れてください。

1. What season do you like?　I like summer.

2. How (　　　　　)[1] CDs do you have?　I have twenty CDs.

3. How much (　　　　　)[2] this bag?　It's 500 yen.

4. Where is the bookstore?　Go straight for (　　　　　)[3] block.

5. Turn left.　You can see it on (　　　　　)[4] right.

6. Can you do this?

7. Why?　I want (　　　　　)[5] eat pizza.

8. What do you do on New Year's Day?　I usually (　　　　　)[6] cards.

9. What do you want for your birthday?　I (　　　　　)[7] a bicycle.

10. What do you want for lunch?　I (　　　　　)[8] a hot dog.

11. What would you like?　I'd (　　　　　)[9] pizza.

12. What is this city famous for?　It's famous for (　　　　　)[10] snow festival.

13. We have the Star Festival in July.

14. You can visit (　　　　　)[11] temple today.　It's beautiful.

15. You can see the festival in August.　It's (　　　　　)[12] interesting.

16. Let's go to India.　India is a nice country.

17. Why（　　　　　）[13] you like India?

18. Are you from Mexico?　No, I'm（　　　　　）[14].

19. We can play baseball at the park.

20. In London,（　　　　　）[15] can ride on a boat on the river.
（　　　　　）[16] can see castles, too.

21. We live in Florida.　We（　　　　　）[17] beautiful beaches.　We can swim in the clear water.　We love Florida（　　　　　）[18] much.

22. Why?　I like my science classes.

23. My name（　　　　　）[19] Mary White.　I saw a lot of taxis in New York.

24. My favorite memory（　　　　　）[20] the summer camp.

eMET 小学 5 年・6 年総合 (4) 問題 日本語訳

問題英文の日本語訳を確認しよう。

1. あなたはどの季節が好きですか。私は夏が好きです。

2. あなたは CD を何枚持っていますか。私は CD を 20 枚持っています。

3. このバッグはいくらですか。500 円です。

4. 本屋はどこですか。1 ブロック直進してください。

5. 左に曲がってください。そうすると，右側に見えます。

6. あなたはこれができますか。

7. なぜですか。ピザが食べたいからです。

8. お正月は何をしますか。私はだいたいトランプをします。

9. 誕生日に何が欲しいですか。自転車が欲しいです。

10. あなたは昼に何が食べたいですか。私はホットドッグが食べたいです。

11. 何にしますか。ピザにします。

12. この都市は何で有名ですか。雪祭りで有名です。

13. 7 月に七夕祭りがあります。

14. 今日そのお寺を訪れることができます。美しいですよ。

15. 8 月にその祭りを見ることができます。とても面白いですよ。

16. インドに行きましょう。インドはすばらしい国です。

17. なぜインドが好きなんですか。

18. あなたはメキシコ出身ですか。いいえ，違います。

19. 私たちは公園で野球をすることができます。

20. ロンドンでは，川で船に乗ることができます。城も見ることができます。

21. 私たちはフロリダに住んでいます。きれいな浜辺があります。澄んだ水の中を泳ぐことができます。私たちはフロリダが大好きです。

22. なぜですか。理科の授業が好きだからです。

23. 私の名前はメアリー・ホワイトです。私はニューヨークでタクシーをたくさん見ました。

24. 私のお気に入りの思い出は夏のキャンプです。

eMET 小学 5 年・6 年総合 (4) 解答

解答付き英文を見ながら，英語の音声をもう一度聞いてみよう。

1. What season do you like?　I like summer.

2. How (**many**)[1] CDs do you have?　I have twenty CDs.

3. How much (**is**)[2] this bag?　It's 500 yen.

4. Where is the bookstore?　Go straight for (**one**)[3] block.

5. Turn left.　You can see it on (**your**)[4] right.

6. Can you do this?

7. Why?　I want (**to**)[5] eat pizza.

8. What do you do on New Year's Day?　I usually (**play**)[6] cards.

9. What do you want for your birthday?　I (**want**)[7] a bicycle.

10. What do you want for lunch?　I (**want**)[8] a hot dog.

11. What would you like?　I'd (**like**)[9] pizza.

12. What is this city famous for?　It's famous for (**its**)[10] snow festival.

13. We have the Star Festival in July.

14. You can visit (**the**)[11] temple today.　It's beautiful.

15. You can see the festival in August.　It's (**very**)[12] interesting.

16. Let's go to India.　India is a nice country.

17. Why (**do**)[13] you like India?

18. Are you from Mexico?　No, I'm (**not**)[14].

19. We can play baseball at the park.

20. In London, (**we**)[15] can ride on a boat on the river.　(**We**)[16] can see castles, too.

21. We live in Florida.　We (**have**)[17] beautiful beaches.　We can swim in the clear water.
    We love Florida (**very**)[18] much.

22. Why?　I like my science classes.

23. My name (**is**)[19] Mary White.　I saw a lot of taxis in New York.

24. My favorite memory (**is**)[20] the summer camp.

第2章

eMET 狭いバージョン問題

　この章には，問題が12題あります。各問題には，空所（　　　）があります。英語の音声を聞きながら，（　　　）の中に，4文字以下（最大で4文字）の英単語を入れてください。

　1題終わるごとに，答え合わせをすることができます。各問題の次のページには，その英文の日本語訳が，そして，その次のページには，解答が太字で示されています。

　答え合わせが終わったら，問題のページに戻り，点数を記入しておくことができます。

eMET 小学 5 年（1）問題

英語の音声を聞きながら，（　　　　　）の中に，4 文字以下（最大で 4 文字）の英単語を入れてください。

1. Look at this photo. This is （　　　　　）^{1} dog.

2. What's your name? My name （　　　　　）^{2} Mary.

3. What sport do you like? I （　　　　　）^{3} tennis.

4. What color do you like? I （　　　　　）^{4} blue.

5. Do you like stories? Yes, （　　　　　）^{5} do.

6. Do you have a ruler? （　　　　　）^{6}, I don't.

7. What do you want （　　　　　）^{7} your birthday? I want a red
    （　　　　　）^{8}.

8. What day is it today? It's Friday.

9. When （　　　　　）^{9} your birthday? My birthday is July 4th.

10. What season （　　　　　）^{10} you like? I like summer.

11. How （　　　　　）^{11} CDs do you have? I have twenty CDs.

12. （　　　　　）^{12} much is this bag? It's 500 yen.

13. Can （　　　　　）^{13} do this? No, I can't.

14. What subject （　　　　　）^{14} you like? I like math.

15. ( )¹⁵ do you want to study? I ( )¹⁶ to study science.

16. What do you want ( )¹⁷ be? I want to be ( )¹⁸ singer.

17. What card do you have? ( )¹⁹ have a baseball card.

18. What do ( )²⁰ do every day? I play in ( )²¹ park every day.

19. Is he a magician? ( )²², he is not.

20. What time ( )²³ you get up? I get ( )²⁴ at seven.

21. After school I eat lunch. Then I ( )²⁵ with my friends.

22. She is a farmer. ( )²⁶ can sing well.

23. He is ( )²⁷ teacher. He is good at baseball.

24. Wash ( )²⁸ hands. Don't push.

eMET 小学 5 年（1）日本語訳

問題英文の日本語訳を確認しよう。

1. この写真を見て。これは，私の犬です。

2. お名前は？　私の名前は，メアリーです。

3. どんなスポーツが好きですか。テニスが好きです。

4. 何色が好きですか。私は青色が好きです。

5. あなたは物語が好きですか。はい，好きです。

6. あなたは定規を持っていますか。いいえ，持っていません。

7. あなたは誕生日に何が欲しいですか。私は赤い帽子が欲しいです。

8. 今日は何曜日ですか。金曜日です。

9. あなたの誕生日はいつですか。私の誕生日は 7 月 4 日です。

10. あなたはどの季節が好きですか。私は夏が好きです。

11. あなたは CD を何枚持っていますか。私は CD を 20 枚持っています。

12. このバッグはいくらですか。500 円です。

13. あなたはこれができますか。いいえ，できません。

14. あなたはどんな科目が好きですか。私は算数が好きです。

15. あなたは何を勉強したいですか。私は理科を勉強したいです。

16. あなたは何になりたいですか。私は歌手になりたいです。

17. どんなカードを持っていますか。私は野球のカードを持っています。

18. あなたは毎日何をしますか。私は毎日公園で遊びます。

19. 彼はマジシャンですか。いいえ，違います。

20. あなたは何時に起きますか。私は 7 時に起きます。

21. 放課後，私は昼ご飯を食べます。その後，友達と遊びます。

22. 彼女は農家です。彼女は歌が上手です。

23. 彼は教師です。彼は野球が上手です。

24. 手を洗ってください。押さないで。

eMET 小学 5 年 (1) 解答

解答付き英文を見ながら，英語の音声をもう一度聞いてみよう。

1. Look at this photo.　This is (**my**)[1] dog.

2. What's your name?　My name (**is**)[2] Mary.

3. What sport do you like?　I (**like**)[3] tennis.

4. What color do you like?　I (**like**)[4] blue.

5. Do you like stories?　Yes, (**I**)[5] do.

6. Do you have a ruler?　(**No**)[6], I don't.

7. What do you want (**for**)[7] your birthday?　I want a red (**cap**)[8].

8. What day is it today?　It's Friday.

9. When (**is**)[9] your birthday?　My birthday is July 4th.

10. What season (**do**)[10] you like?　I like summer.

11. How (**many**)[11] CDs do you have?　I have twenty CDs.

12. (**How**)[12] much is this bag?　It's 500 yen.

13. Can (**you**)[13] do this?　No, I can't.

14. What subject (**do**)[14] you like?　I like math.

15. (**What**)[15] do you want to study?　I (**want**)[16] to study science.

16. What do you want (**to**)[17] be?　I want to be (**a**)[18] singer.

17. What card do you have?　(**I**)[19] have a baseball card.

18. What do (**you**)[20] do every day?　I play in (**the**)[21] park every day.

19. Is he a magician?　(**No**)[22], he is not.

20. What time (**do**)[23] you get up?　I get (**up**)[24] at seven.

21. After school I eat lunch.　Then I (**play**)[25] with my friends.

22. She is a farmer.　(**She**)[26] can sing well.

23. He is (**a**)[27] teacher.　He is good at baseball.

24. Wash (**your**)[28] hands.　Don't push.

eMET 小学 5 年 (2) 問題

英語の音声を聞きながら, ( ) の中に, 4 文字以下 (最大で 4 文字) の英単語を入れてください。

1. Can you cook well?　Yes, (　　　　　)^1 can.　He can cook curry and (　　　　　)^2 well.

2. Who is Mary White?　She is (　　　　　)^3 friend.　She is a baker.

3. Where is my (　　　　　)^4?

4. What time do you get (　　　　　)^5?　I usually get up at five.

5. Are (　　　　　)^6 happy?　Yes, I am.

6. She is (　　　　　)^7 sister.

7. He is Bill.　He can swim (　　　　　)^8.　He can't run fast.

8. Who is (　　　　　)^9?　This is Kate.

9. Where is the racket?　It's by (　　　　　)^{10} desk.

10. Where is your book?　You (　　　　　)^{11} see it on your left.

11. (　　　　　)^{12} can you do?　I can (　　　　　)^{13} fast.

12. Are you good at cooking?　(　　　　　)^{14}, I'm not.

13. Where is the bookstore?　Go straight for (　　　　　)^{15} block.

14. Turn left.　You can see (　　　　　)^{16} on your right.

15. Can you do (　　　　　)^{17}?

16. I can play the violin.

17. Can ( )[18] swim?

18. She can play the guitar.

19. ( )[19] want bananas.

20. I eat dinner at six.

21. She ( )[20] sing well.

22. She can't play the guitar.

23. ( )[21] can skate well.

24. Don't go!

eMET 小学 5 年 (2) 問題 日本語訳

問題英文の日本語訳を確認しよう。

1. 料理を上手に作ることができますか。はい，できます。彼はカレーライスを上手に作ることができます。

2. メアリー・ホワイトって，誰ですか。彼女は私の友達です。彼女はパン屋です。

3. 私の本はどこですか。

4. あなたは何時に起きますか。私は普段 5 時に起きます。

5. あなたは幸せですか。はい，幸せです。

6. 彼女は私の妹です。

7. 彼はビルです。彼は速く泳ぐことができます。彼は速く走ることができません。

8. これは誰ですか。これはケイトです。

9. ラケットはどこですか。机のそばです。

10. あなたの本はどこですか。あなたの左側にあります。

11. あなたは何ができますか。私は速く走ることができます。

12. あなたは料理が上手ですか。いいえ，上手じゃありません。

13. 本屋はどこですか。1 ブロック直進してください。

14. 左に曲がってください。そうすると，右側に見えます。

15. あなたはこれができますか。

16. 私はバイオリンを弾くことができます。

17. 彼女は泳げますか。

18. 彼女はギターを弾くことができます。

19. 私はバナナが欲しいです。

20. 私は 6 時に晩ご飯を食べます。

21. 彼女は歌が上手です。

22. 彼女はギターが弾けません。

23. 彼女はスケートが上手です。

24. 行ったらだめです。

eMET 小学 5 年（2）解答

解答付き英文を見ながら，英語の音声をもう一度聞いてみよう。

1. Can you cook well?   Yes, (**I**)[1] can.   He can cook curry and (**rice**)[2] well.

2. Who is Mary White?   She is (**my**)[3] friend.   She is a baker.

3. Where is my (**book**)[4]?

4. What time do you get (**up**)[5]?   I usually get up at five.

5. Are (**you**)[6] happy?   Yes, I am.

6. She is (**my**)[7] sister.

7. He is Bill.   He can swim (**fast**)[8].   He can't run fast.

8. Who is (**this**)[9]?   This is Kate.

9. Where is the racket?   It's by (**the**)[10] desk.

10. Where is your book?   You (**can**)[11] see it on your left.

11. (**What**)[12] can you do?   I can (**run**)[13] fast.

12. Are you good at cooking?   (**No**)[14], I'm not.

13. Where is the bookstore?   Go straight for (**one**)[15] block.

14. Turn left.   You can see (**it**)[16] on your right.

15. Can you do (**this**)[17]?

16. I can play the violin.

17. Can (**she**)[18] swim?

18. She can play the guitar.

19. (**I**)[19] want bananas.

20. I eat dinner at six.

21. She (**can**)[20] sing well.

22. She can't play the guitar.

23. (**She**)[21] can skate well.

24. Don't go!

eMET 小学 5 年 (3) 問題

英語の音声を聞きながら,（　　　　　）の中に, 4 文字以下（最大で 4 文字）の英単語を入れてください。

1. What would you like?　I'd like a hamburger.

2. (　　　　　)^1 food do you like?　I (　　　　　)^2 French fries.

3. How much is it?　A hamburger (　　　　　)^3 300 yen.

4. This is an apple.　It's delicious.

5. This is Miss Green.　(　　　　　)^4 is a soccer player.

6. She can run (　　　　　)^5.

7. Look at this picture.　This is Mr. Green.

8. (　　　　　)^6 he good at cooking?　Yes, he (　　　　　)^7.

9. Is he your hero?　Yes, (　　　　　)^8 is.

10. Is she a junior high school student?　(　　　　　)^9, she is.

11. She can dance very (　　　　　)^{10}.　That's great!

12. Can he fly a kite?　(　　　　　)^{11}, he can.

13. Where is the cat?　(　　　　　)^{12} is on the box.

14. Where is (　　　　　)^{13} fox?　It is in the (　　　　　)^{14}.

15. Where do you want to go?　(　　　　　)^{15} want to go to Italy.

16. Why?　(　　　　　)^{16} want to eat pizza.

17. What do (   )^{17} do on New Year's Day?   I usually (   )^{18} cards.

18. What do you want for (   )^{19} birthday?   I want a bicycle.

19. This is (   )^{20} original menu.

20. I want to go (   )^{21} Boston.

21. I want to see Susan.

22. Do (   )^{22} help your parents?

23. What do you (   )^{23}?   I like robots.   I'm in the robot club (   )^{24} school.

24. Where's the flower shop?   Go straight.   Turn right at (   )^{25} park.

eMET 小学 5 年（3）問題 日本語訳

問題英文の日本語訳を確認しよう。

1. 何にしますか。ハンバーガーにします。

2. あなたはどんな食べ物が好きですか。私はフライドポテトが好きです。

3. それはいくらですか。ハンバーガーは 300 円です。

4. これはリンゴです。おいしいですよ。

5. これはグリーンさんです。彼女はサッカー選手です。

6. 彼女は速く走ることができます。

7. この絵を見て。これはグリーンさんです。

8. 彼は料理が上手ですか。はい。

9. 彼はあなたの憧れですか。はい。

10. 彼女は中学生ですか。はい。

11. 彼女は上手に踊ることができます。それはすばらしい。

12. 彼は凧をあげることができますか。はい，できます。

13. 猫はどこですか。箱の上にいます。

14. キツネはどこですか。箱の中です。

15. あなたはどこに行きたいですか。私はイタリアに行きたいです。

16. なぜですか。ピザが食べたいからです。

17. お正月は何をしますか。私はだいたいトランプをします。

18. 誕生日に何が欲しいですか。自転車が欲しいです。

19. これは私のオリジナルメニューです。

20. 私はボストンに行きたいです。

21. 私はスーザンに会いたいです。

22. あなたは両親の手伝いをしますか。

23. あなたは何が好きですか。私はロボットが好きです。私は学校でロボットクラブに所属しています。

24. 花屋はどこですか。まっすぐ進んでください。公園を右に曲がってください。

eMET 小学 5 年（3）解答

解答付き英文を見ながら，英語の音声をもう一度聞いてみよう。

1. What would you like?　I'd like a hamburger.

2. （ **What**)[1] food do you like?　I (**like**)[2] French fries.

3. How much is it?　A hamburger (**is**)[3] 300 yen.

4. This is an apple.　It's delicious.

5. This is Miss Green.　(**She**)[4] is a soccer player.

6. She can run (**fast**)[5].

7. Look at this picture.　This is Mr. Green.

8. (**Is**)[6] he good at cooking?　Yes, he (**is**)[7].

9. Is he your hero?　Yes, (**he**)[8] is.

10. Is she a junior high school student?　(**Yes**)[9], she is.

11. She can dance very (**well**)[10].　That's great!

12. Can he fly a kite?　(**Yes**)[11], he can.

13. Where is the cat?　(**It**)[12] is on the box.

14. Where is (**the**)[13] fox?　It is in the (**box**)[14].

15. Where do you want to go?　(**I**)[15] want to go to Italy.

16. Why?　(**I**)[16] want to eat pizza.

17. What do (**you**)[17] do on New Year's Day?　I usually (**play**)[18] cards.

18. What do you want for (**your**)[19] birthday?　I want a bicycle.

19. This is (**my**)[20] original menu.

20. I want to go (**to**)[21] Boston.

21. I want to see Susan.

22. Do (**you**)[22] help your parents?

23. What do you (**like**)[23]?　I like robots.　I'm in the robot club (**at**)[24] school.

24. Where's the flower shop?　Go straight.　Turn right at (**the**)[25] park.

eMET 小学 5 年（4）問題

英語の音声を聞きながら，（　　　　）の中に，4 文字以下（最大で 4 文字）の英単語を入れてください。

1. My name is Kate. I like singing.

2. (　　　　)[1] hero is my English teacher. He can (　　　　)[2] very well.

3. He is a (　　　　)[3] good teacher.

4. Who is your hero? (　　　　)[4] hero is my brother.

5. Why is (　　　　)[5] your hero? He is good (　　　　)[6] cooking.

6. He is always kind to me.

7. (　　　　)[7] you good at playing soccer? Yes, I (　　　　)[8].

8. What would you like? I'd like spaghetti.

9. How (　　　　)[9] is the spaghetti? It's 500 yen.

10. Where do you want (　　　　)[10] go? I want to go (　　　　)[11] the amusement park.

11. I want to (　　　　)[12] to the beach.

12. Where is the station? Go straight. (　　　　)[13] right at the second corner.

13. You can see (　　　　)[14] on your right.

14. This is Miss Davis. She (　　　　　　)¹⁵ swim very fast. She is (　　　　　　)¹⁶. She is my favorite swimmer.

15. Where do you (　　　　　　)¹⁷ to go? I want to (　　　　　　)¹⁸ to Africa.

16. This is Mr. Brown.　He is a firefighter.

17. (　　　　　　)¹⁹ is your best friend?　My best friend (　　　　　　)²⁰ Kate.

18. She is a police officer.

19. What do (　　　　　　)²¹ want for lunch?　I want a (　　　　　　)²² dog.

20. What would you like?　I'd like pizza.

21. What (　　　　　　)²³ this city famous for?　It's famous for its (　　　　　　)²⁴ festival.

22. What is the town famous for?　It's famous for (　　　　　　)²⁵ beef.

23. What is your city famous for?　(　　　　　　)²⁶ city is famous for its castle.

24. I (　　　　　　)²⁷ to see a rocket.

eMET 小学 5 年（4）問題 日本語訳

問題英文の日本語訳を確認しよう。

1. 私の名前はケイトです。私は歌うことが好きです。

2. 私の憧れの人は，私の英語の先生です。彼は歌がとても上手です。

3. 彼はとても良い先生です。

4. 憧れの人は誰ですか。兄です。

5. なぜ彼はあなたの憧れですか。料理が上手だからです。

6. 彼はいつも私に親切です。

7. あなたはサッカーが得意ですか。はい，得意です。

8. 何にしますか。スパゲッティにします。

9. スパゲッティはいくらしますか。500 円です。

10. どこに行きたいですか。私は遊園地に行きたいです。

11. 私は海に行きたいです。

12. 駅はどこですか。まっすぐ進んでください。2 つ目の角を右に曲がってください。

13. あなたの右側にそれが見えます。

14. これはデイビスさんです。彼女はとても速く泳ぐことができます。彼女はかっこいいです。彼女は私のお気に入りの水泳選手です。

15. あなたはどこに行きたいですか。私はアフリカに行きたいです。

16. これはブラウンさんです。彼は消防士です。

17. あなたの一番の友達は誰ですか。私の一番の友達はケイトです。

18. 彼女は警官です。

19. あなたは昼に何が食べたいですか。私はホットドッグが食べたいです。

20. 何にしますか。ピザにします。

21. この都市は何で有名ですか。雪祭りで有名です。

22. その町は何で有名ですか。牛肉で有名です。

23. あなたの市は何で有名ですか。私の市は城で有名です。

24. 私はロケットが見たいです。

eMET 小学 5 年（4）解答

解答付き英文を見ながら，英語の音声をもう一度聞いてみよう。

1. My name is Kate.　I like singing.

2. （ **My**)[1] hero is my English teacher.　He can（ **sing**)[2] very well.

3. He is a（ **very**)[3] good teacher.

4. Who is your hero?　（ **My**)[4] hero is my brother.

5. Why is（ **he**)[5] your hero?　He is good（ **at**)[6] cooking.

6. He is always kind to me.

7. （ **Are**)[7] you good at playing soccer?　Yes, I（ **am**)[8].

8. What would you like?　I'd like spaghetti.

9. How（ **much**)[9] is the spaghetti?　It's 500 yen.

10. Where do you want（ **to**)[10] go?　I want to go（ **to**)[11] the amusement park.

11. I want to（ **go**)[12] to the beach.

12. Where is the station?　Go straight.　（ **Turn**)[13] right at the second corner.

13. You can see（ **it**)[14] on your right.

14. This is Miss Davis.　She（ **can**)[15] swim very fast.　She is（ **cool**)[16].　She is my favorite swimmer.

15. Where do you（ **want**)[17] to go?　I want to（ **go**)[18] to Africa.

16. This is Mr. Brown.　He is a firefighter.

17. （ **Who**)[19] is your best friend?　My best friend（ **is**)[20] Kate.

18. She is a police officer.

19. What do（ **you**)[21] want for lunch?　I want a（ **hot**)[22] dog.

20. What would you like?　I'd like pizza.

21. What（ **is**)[23] this city famous for?　It's famous for its（ **snow**)[24] festival.

22. What is the town famous for?　It's famous for（ **its**)[25] beef.

23. What is your city famous for?　（ **My**)[26] city is famous for its castle.

24. I（ **want**)[27] to see a rocket.

eMET 小学 6 年（1）問題

英語の音声を聞きながら，（　　　　　）の中に，4 文字以下（最大で 4 文字）の英単語を入れてください。

1. I'm Emily. I'm from Spain.

2. Where are you from?

3. What animals （　　　　　）^{1} you like? I like dogs.

4. （　　　　　）^{2} is your birthday? My birthday is May 4th.

5. （　　　　　）^{3} can play the recorder well. That's great!

6. My （　　　　　）^{4} is John. I'm from Canada.

7. I like music. I （　　　　　）^{5} play the piano.

8. My favorite place is the music （　　　　　）^{6}.

9. I'm good at painting pictures.

10. Is there anything that we （　　　　　）^{7} do for you?

11. What's your favorite sport? My favorite sport （　　　　　）^{8} baseball.

12. Where do you live? I live （　　　　　）^{9} France.

13. I'm from London.

14. I'm good at singing.

15. What fruit do （　　　　　）^{10} like? I like oranges.

16. What vegetable do （　　　　　）^{11} like? I like tomatoes.

17. Welcome to my （　　　　　）^{12}.

18. My town is beautiful.　We have （　　　　　）^{13} big park.

19. We can enjoy fishing.

20. In summer, （　　　　　）^{14} have a summer festival.　You can enjoy delicious food.　（　　　　　）^{15} can enjoy dancing, too.

21. We have an entrance ceremony （　　　　　）^{16} April.　We don't have an entrance ceremony in September.

22. We （　　　　　）^{17} the Star Festival in July.

23. You can visit （　　　　　）^{18} temple today.　It's beautiful.

24. You can see the festival in August.　It's （　　　　　）^{19} interesting.

eMET 小学 6 年 (1) 問題 日本語訳

問題英文の日本語訳を確認しよう。

1. 私はエミリーです。私はスペイン出身です。

2. あなたの出身地はどこですか。

3. どんな動物が好きですか。私は犬が好きです。

4. あなたの誕生日はいつですか。私の誕生日は 5 月 4 日です。

5. 私はリコーダーを上手に演奏できます。すばらしいですね。

6. 私の名前はジョンです。私はカナダ出身です。

7. 私は音楽が好きです。私はピアノを弾くことができます。

8. 私のお気に入りの場所は音楽室です。

9. 私は絵を描くことが得意です。

10. あなたのために何かできることはありますか。

11. あなたのお気に入りのスポーツは何ですか。私のお気に入りのスポーツは野球です。

12. どこに住んでいますか。私はフランスに住んでいます。

13. 私はロンドン出身です。

14. 私は歌うことが得意です。

15. あなたはどんな果物が好きですか。私はオレンジが好きです。

16. あなたはどんな野菜が好きですか。私はトマトが好きです。

17. 私の町へようこそ。

18. 私の町は美しいです。大きい公園があります。

19. 私たちは釣りを楽しむことができます。

20. 夏には，夏祭りがあります。おいしい食べ物を食べることができます。踊りを楽しむこともできます。

21. 私たちは 4 月に入学式があります。9 月には入学式がありません。

22. 7 月に七夕祭りがあります。

23. 今日そのお寺を訪れることができます。美しいですよ。

24. 8 月にその祭りを見ることができます。とても面白いですよ。

eMET 小学 6 年（1）解答

解答付き英文を見ながら，英語の音声をもう一度聞いてみよう。

1. I'm Emily. I'm from Spain.

2. Where are you from?

3. What animals (**do**)[1] you like? I like dogs.

4. (**When**)[2] is your birthday? My birthday is May 4th.

5. (**I**)[3] can play the recorder well. That's great!

6. My (**name**)[4] is John. I'm from Canada.

7. I like music. I (**can**)[5] play the piano.

8. My favorite place is the music (**room**)[6].

9. I'm good at painting pictures.

10. Is there anything that we (**can**)[7] do for you?

11. What's your favorite sport? My favorite sport (**is**)[8] baseball.

12. Where do you live? I live (**in**)[9] France.

13. I'm from London.

14. I'm good at singing.

15. What fruit do (**you**)[10] like? I like oranges.

16. What vegetable do (**you**)[11] like? I like tomatoes.

17. Welcome to my (**town**)[12].

18. My town is beautiful. We have (**a**)[13] big park.

19. We can enjoy fishing.

20. In summer, (**we**)[14] have a summer festival. You can enjoy delicious food. (**You**)[15] can enjoy dancing, too.

21. We have an entrance ceremony (**in**)[16] April. We don't have an entrance ceremony in September.

22. We (**have**)[17] the Star Festival in July.

23. You can visit (**the**)[18] temple today. It's beautiful.

24. You can see the festival in August. It's (**very**)[19] interesting.

eMET 小学 6 年（2）問題

英語の音声を聞きながら，（　　　　　）の中に，4 文字以下（最大で 4 文字）の英単語を入れてください。

1. Let's go to India.　India is a nice country.

2. (　　　　　　)^1 do you like India?

3. Are you (　　　　　　)^2 Mexico?　No, I'm not.

4. Where do you want (　　　　　)^3 go?　I want to go (　　　　　)^4 Canada.

5. You can enjoy the flowers in May.

6. (　　　　　　)^5 can eat lunch under the trees.

7. Can I (　　　　　　)^6?　No, you can't.

8. Let's watch volleyball together.

9. I want to watch table tennis.　It's exciting.

10. (　　　　　　)^7 is our town.　We have (　　　　　)^8 nice library.　We have a zoo.

11. (　　　　　　)^9 do you want in our (　　　　　)^{10}?　I want a museum.

12. I'm Michael.　I'm from Australia.

13. I (　　　　　　)^{11} Japanese food.　I like reading Japanese books.

14. Where did you (　　　　　)^{12} this summer?　I went to the beach.

15. (   )[13] was your summer vacation? It was great. I enjoyed camping.

16. (   )[14] can climb the mountain. It's very beautiful. Please try it.

17. (   )[15] you a giraffe?   Yes, I am.

18. (   )[16] can play with the elephants.

19. You can (   )[17] good tea.

20. You can visit the (   )[18] by boat.

21. Let's sing a song.

22. Let's (   )[19] the cake.

23. I am tall.

24. (   )[20] have long legs.

eMET 小学 6 年（2）問題 日本語訳

問題英文の日本語訳を確認しよう。

1. インドに行きましょう。インドはすばらしい国です。

2. なぜインドが好きなんですか。

3. あなたはメキシコ出身ですか。いいえ，違います。

4. あなたはどこに行きたいですか。私はカナダに行きたいです。

5. 5月に花を楽しむことができます。

6. 木の下でお昼を食べることができます。

7. 私は行けますか。いいえ，行けません。

8. 一緒にバレーボールを見ましょう。

9. 私は卓球が見たいです。わくわくさせてくれますよね。

10. これは私たちの町です。すばらしい図書館があります。動物園があります。

11. 私たちの町に何が欲しいですか。私は博物館が欲しいです。

12. 私はマイケルです。私はオーストラリア出身です。

13. 私は日本食が好きです。私は日本の本を読むことが好きです。

14. この夏，あなたはどこに行きましたか。私は海に行きました。

15. 夏休みはどうでしたか。よかったですよ。キャンプを楽しみました。

16. その山に登ることができます。とても美しいですよ。試してみてください。

17. あなたはキリンですか。はい，そうです。

18. 象と遊ぶことができます。

19. いいお茶が買えますよ。

20. あなたは船でその都市を訪れることができます。

21. 歌を歌いましょう。

22. ケーキを切りましょう。

23. 私は背が高いです。

24. 私は足が長いです。

eMET 小学 6 年（2）解答

解答付き英文を見ながら，英語の音声をもう一度聞いてみよう。

1. Let's go to India. India is a nice country.

2. (**Why**)[1] do you like India?

3. Are you (**from**)[2] Mexico? No, I'm not.

4. Where do you want (**to**)[3] go? I want to go (**to**)[4] Canada.

5. You can enjoy the flowers in May.

6. (**You**)[5] can eat lunch under the trees.

7. Can I (**go**)[6]? No, you can't.

8. Let's watch volleyball together.

9. I want to watch table tennis. It's exciting.

10. (**This**)[7] is our town. We have (**a**)[8] nice library. We have a zoo.

11. (**What**)[9] do you want in our (**town**)[10]? I want a museum.

12. I'm Michael. I'm from Australia.

13. I (**like**)[11] Japanese food. I like reading Japanese books.

14. Where did you (**go**)[12] this summer? I went to the beach.

15. (**How**)[13] was your summer vacation? It was great. I enjoyed camping.

16. (**You**)[14] can climb the mountain. It's very beautiful. Please try it.

17. (**Are**)[15] you a giraffe? Yes, I am.

18. (**You**)[16] can play with the elephants.

19. You can (**buy**)[17] good tea.

20. You can visit the (**city**)[18] by boat.

21. Let's sing a song.

22. Let's (**cut**)[19] the cake.

23. I am tall.

24. (**I**)[20] have long legs.

eMET 小学 **6** 年 (3) 問題

英語の音声を聞きながら, ( ) の中に, 4 文字以下 (最大で 4 文字) の英単語を入れてください。

1. Where do dolphins live? They live in (   )[1] sea.

2. Where do lions live? They live (   )[2] the savanna.

3. We can read English books (   )[3] the library.

4. We can play baseball at (   )[4] park.

5. In London, we can ride (   )[5] a boat on the river. We
   (   )[6] see castles, too.

6. We live in Florida. (   )[7] have beautiful beaches. We can
   swim in (   )[8] clear water. We love Florida very much.

7. What country (   )[9] you want to visit? I want (   )[10]
   visit France.

8. Why? I want to see (   )[11] castle.

9. You can eat French bread. It's delicious.

10. He is (   )[12] athlete.

11. He is from Brazil. He can (   )[13] tennis very well. He is
    famous.

12. What (   )[14] you do yesterday? I played tennis yesterday.

13. What did (　　　　　　　)^{15} do last weekend? I played soccer last Sunday. It (　　　　　　　)^{16} exciting.

14. Are you hungry? I usually eat beef curry (　　　　　　　)^{17} home.

15. Where is the beef from? (　　　　　　　)^{18} is from Australia.

16. Where do you want (　　　　　　　)^{19} go? I want to go (　　　　　　　)^{20} the bank.

17. Go straight. Turn right at (　　　　　　　)^{21} first corner.

18. What do you want to (　　　　　　　)^{22}? I want to be a carpenter.

19. (　　　　　　　)^{23} want to build a house.

20. What is (　　　　　　　)^{24} best memory? My best memory is the school (　　　　)^{25}.

21. We went to China in January.

22. What (　　　　　　　)^{26} you see? We saw a (　　　　　　　)^{27} of temples.

23. I want to see (　　　　　　　)^{28} singer.

24. I want to go to (　　　　　　　)^{29} zoo.

eMET 小学 6 年（3）問題 日本語訳

問題英文の日本語訳を確認しよう。

1. イルカはどこに住んでいますか。海に住んでいます。

2. ライオンはどこに住んでいますか。サバンナに住んでいます。

3. 私たちは図書館で英語の本を読むことができます。

4. 私たちは公園で野球をすることができます。

5. ロンドンでは，川で船に乗ることができます。城も見ることができます。

6. 私たちはフロリダに住んでいます。きれいな浜辺があります。澄んだ水の中を泳ぐことができます。私たちはフロリダが大好きです。

7. あなたはどの国を訪れたいですか。私はフランスを訪れたいです。

8. なぜですか。城が見たいからです。

9. フランスパンを食べることができます。とてもおいしいですよ。

10. 彼はアスリートです。

11. 彼はブラジル出身です。彼はとても上手にテニスをすることができます。彼は有名です。

12. 昨日何をしましたか。私は昨日テニスをしました。

13. 先週末は何をしましたか。私は先週の日曜日にサッカーをしました。とても楽しかったです。

14. 腹ペコですか。私は普段家でビーフカレーを食べます。

15. そのビーフはどこから来ていますか。オーストラリアです。

16. あなたはどこに行きたいですか。銀行に行きたいです。

17. まっすぐ進んでください。最初の角を右に曲がってください。

18. あなたは何になりたいですか。私は大工になりたいです。

19. 私は家を建てたいです。

20. あなたの一番の思い出は何ですか。私の一番の思い出は修学旅行です。

21. 私たちは 1 月に中国に行きました。

22. 何を見ましたか。お寺をたくさん見ました。

23. 私はその歌手を見たいです。

24. 私は動物園に行きたいです。

eMET 小学 6 年 (3) 解答

解答付き英文を見ながら，英語の音声をもう一度聞いてみよう。

1. Where do dolphins live?　They live in（ **the**)[1] sea.

2. Where do lions live?　They live（ **in**)[2] the savanna.

3. We can read English books（ **in**)[3] the library.

4. We can play baseball at（ **the**)[4] park.

5. In London, we can ride（ **on**)[5] a boat on the river.　We（ **can**)[6] see castles, too.

6. We live in Florida.　（ **We**)[7] have beautiful beaches.　We can swim in（ **the**)[8] clear water.　We love Florida very much.

7. What country（ **do**)[9] you want to visit?　I want（ **to**)[10] visit France.

8. Why?　I want to see（ **the**)[11] castle.

9. You can eat French bread.　It's delicious.

10. He is（ **an**)[12] athlete.

11. He is from Brazil.　He can（ **play**)[13] tennis very well.　He is famous.

12. What（ **did**)[14] you do yesterday?　I played tennis yesterday.

13. What did（ **you**)[15] do last weekend?　I played soccer last Sunday.　It（ **was**)[16] exciting.

14. Are you hungry?　I usually eat beef curry（ **at**)[17] home.

15. Where is the beef from?　（ **It**)[18] is from Australia.

16. Where do you want（ **to**)[19] go?　I want to go（ **to**)[20] the bank.

17. Go straight.　Turn right at（ **the**)[21] first corner.

18. What do you want to（ **be**)[22]?　I want to be a carpenter.

19. （ **I**)[23] want to build a house.

20. What is（ **your**)[24] best memory?　My best memory is the school（ **trip**)[25].

21. We went to China in January.

22. What（ **did**)[26] you see?　We saw a（ **lot**)[27] of temples.

23. I want to see（ **the**)[28] singer.

24. I want to go to（ **the**)[29] zoo.

eMET 小学 **6** 年 (4) 問題

英語の音声を聞きながら，(　　　　) の中に，4 文字以下 (最大で 4 文字) の英単語を入れてください。

1. What club do you want (　　　　)^1 join?　I want to join (　　　　)^2 volleyball club.

2. What school event do you want (　　　　)^3 enjoy?　I want to enjoy sports day.

3. What (　　　　)^4 you want to be?　I (　　　　)^5 to be a teacher.

4. Who is (　　　　)^6 favorite sports player?　My favorite sports player is Michael Jordan.

5. He is a (　　　　)^7 basketball player.

6. I'm Fred.　I want to be a scientist.

7. (　　　　)^8?　I like my science classes.

8. My name (　　　　)^9 Mary White.　I saw a lot of taxis (　　　　)^{10} New York.

9. My favorite memory is the summer camp.

10. I (　　　　)^{11} to the zoo.　I saw pandas.

11. (　　　　)^{12} enjoyed taking pictures.

12. I ate a hamburger.

13. Who is (　　　　)^{13}?　He is Bill, a famous artist.

14. He can (　　　　　　　)^{14} and dance very well.

15. Who is (　　　　　　　)^{15}?　This is Kate.　She is from Korea.

16. (　　　　　　　)^{16} do you want to enjoy?　I (　　　　　　　)^{17} to enjoy the chorus contest.

17. What club do (　　　　　　)^{18} want to join?　I like music.

18. (　　　　　　　)^{19} can play the drums.　I want to (　　　　　　)^{20} the brass band.

19. What club do (　　　　　)^{21} want to join?　I want (　　　　　)^{22} join the science club.　Me, too.

20. (　　　　　　)^{23} do you want to be?　(　　　　　　)^{24} want to be a soccer player.

21. I (　　　　　　)^{25} soccer.

22. What club do you want (　　　　　　)^{26} join? I want to join (　　　　　)^{27} cooking club.

23. What subject do you want (　　　　　)^{28} study hard?　I want to study math (　　　　　)^{29}.

24. We have many events and activities in junior (　　　　　　)^{30} school life.

eMET 小学 6 年（4）問題 日本語訳

問題英文の日本語訳を確認しよう。

1. あなたはどのクラブに入りたいですか。私はバレーボールクラブに入りたいです。

2. あなたはどんな学校行事を楽しみたいですか。体育祭を楽しみたいです。

3. あなたは何になりたいですか。先生になりたいです。

4. あなたのお気に入りのスポーツ選手は誰ですか。私のお気に入りのスポーツ選手は，マイケル・ジョーダンです。

5. 彼はすばらしいバスケットボール選手です。

6. 私はフレッドです。私は科学者になりたいです。

7. なぜですか。理科の授業が好きだからです。

8. 私の名前はメアリー・ホワイトです。私はニューヨークでタクシーをたくさん見ました。

9. 私のお気に入りの思い出は夏のキャンプです。

10. 私は動物園に行きました。私はパンダを見ました。

11. 私は写真を撮って楽しみました。

12. 私はハンバーガーを食べました。

13. これは誰ですか。彼はビルで，有名なアーティストです。

14. 彼はとても上手に歌って踊れます。

15. これは誰ですか。これはケイトです。彼女は韓国出身です。

16. あなたは何を楽しみたいですか。合唱コンクールを楽しみたいです。

17. あなたはどのクラブに入りたいですか。私は音楽が好きです。

18. 私はドラムを演奏することができます。私は吹奏楽部に入りたいです。

19. あなたは何クラブに入りたいですか。私は理科クラブに入りたいです。私もです。

20. あなたは何になりたいですか。私はサッカー選手になりたいです。

21. 私はサッカーが好きです。

22. あなたはどんなクラブに入りたいですか。私は料理クラブに入りたいです。

23. あなたはどんな科目を一所懸命勉強したいですか。私は算数を一所懸命勉強したいです。

24. 中学校生活にはたくさんの行事と活動があります。

eMET 小学 6 年 (4) 解答

解答付き英文を見ながら，英語の音声をもう一度聞いてみよう。

1. What club do you want (**to**)¹ join?　I want to join (**the**)² volleyball club.

2. What school event do you want (**to**)³ enjoy?　I want to enjoy sports day.

3. What (**do**)⁴ you want to be?　I (**want**)⁵ to be a teacher.

4. Who is (**your**)⁶ favorite sports player?　My favorite sports player is Michael Jordan.

5. He is a (**good**)⁷ basketball player.

6. I'm Fred.　I want to be a scientist.

7. (**Why**)⁸?　I like my science classes.

8. My name (**is**)⁹ Mary White.　I saw a lot of taxis (**in**)¹⁰ New York.

9. My favorite memory is the summer camp.

10. I (**went**)¹¹ to the zoo.　I saw pandas.

11. (**I**)¹² enjoyed taking pictures.

12. I ate a hamburger.

13. Who is (**this**)¹³?　He is Bill, a famous artist.

14. He can (**sing**)¹⁴ and dance very well.

15. Who is (**this**)¹⁵?　This is Kate.　She is from Korea.

16. (**What**)¹⁶ do you want to enjoy?　I (**want**)¹⁷ to enjoy the chorus contest.

17. What club do (**you**)¹⁸ want to join?　I like music.

18. (**I**)¹⁹ can play the drums.　I want to (**join**)²⁰ the brass band.

19. What club do (**you**)²¹ want to join?　I want (**to**)²² join the science club.　Me, too.

20. (**What**)²³ do you want to be?　(**I**)²⁴ want to be a soccer player.

21. I (**like**)²⁵ soccer.

22. What club do you want (**to**)²⁶ join?　I want to join (**the**)²⁷ cooking club.

23. What subject do you want (**to**)²⁸ study hard?　I want to study math (**hard**)²⁹.

24. We have many events and activities in junior (**high**)³⁰ school life.

eMET 小学 5 年・6 年総合 (1) 問題

英語の音声を聞きながら, ( ) の中に, 4 文字以下 (最大で 4 文字) の英単語を入れてください。

1. Look at this photo.   This is ( )^1 dog.

2. What's your name?   My name ( )^2 Mary.

3. What sport do you like?   I ( )^3 tennis.

4. What time do you get ( )^4?   I usually get up at five.

5. ( )^5 you happy?   Yes, I am.

6. She ( )^6 my sister.

7. Look at this picture.   This ( )^7 Mr. Green.

8. Is he good at cooking?   Yes, ( )^8 is.

9. Is he your hero?   ( )^9, he is.

10. Where do you want ( )^{10} go?   I want to go ( )^{11} the amusement park.

11. I want to ( )^{12} to the beach.

12. Where is the station?   Go straight.   ( )^{13} right at the second corner.

13. I'm from London.

14. I'm ( )^{14} at singing.

15. What fruit do you like?   (   )^{15} like oranges.

16. You can climb the mountain.   It's very beautiful.   Please (   )^{16} it.

17. Are you a giraffe?   Yes, (   )^{17} am.

18. You can play with the elephants.

19. (   )^{18} want to build a house.

20. What is (   )^{19} best memory?   My best memory is the school (   )^{20}.

21. We went to China in January.

22. What (   )^{21} do you want to join?   (   )^{22} want to join the cooking club.

23. (   )^{23} subject do you want to study hard?   (   )^{24} want to study math hard.

24. We (   )^{25} many events and activities in junior high school life.

eMET 小学 5 年・6 年総合（1）問題 日本語訳

問題英文の日本語訳を確認しよう。

1. この写真を見て。これは，私の犬です。

2. お名前は？　私の名前は，メアリーです。

3. どんなスポーツが好きですか。テニスが好きです。

4. あなたは何時に起きますか。私は普段 5 時に起きます。

5. あなたは幸せですか。はい，幸せです。

6. 彼女は私の妹です。

7. この絵を見て。これはグリーンさんです。

8. 彼は料理が上手ですか。はい。

9. 彼はあなたの憧れですか。はい。

10. どこに行きたいですか。私は遊園地に行きたいです。

11. 私は海に行きたいです。

12. 駅はどこですか。まっすぐ進んでください。2 つ目の角を右に曲がってください。

13. 私はロンドン出身です。

14. 私は歌うことが得意です。

15. あなたはどんな果物が好きですか。私はオレンジが好きです。

16. その山に登ることができます。とても美しいですよ。試してみてください。

17. あなたはキリンですか。はい，そうです。

18. 象と遊ぶことができます。

19. 私は家を建てたいです。

20. あなたの一番の思い出は何ですか。私の一番の思い出は修学旅行です。

21. 私たちは 1 月に中国に行きました。

22. あなたはどんなクラブに入りたいですか。私は料理クラブに入りたいです。

23. あなたはどんな科目を一所懸命勉強したいですか。私は算数を一所懸命勉強したいです。

24. 中学校生活にはたくさんの行事と活動があります。

eMET 小学 5 年・6 年総合（1）解答

解答付き英文を見ながら，英語の音声をもう一度聞いてみよう。

1. Look at this photo.　This is（ **my**)[1] dog.

2. What's your name?　My name（ **is**)[2] Mary.

3. What sport do you like?　I（ **like**)[3] tennis.

4. What time do you get（ **up**)[4]?　I usually get up at five.

5. （ **Are**)[5] you happy?　Yes, I am.

6. She（ **is**)[6] my sister.

7. Look at this picture.　This（ **is**)[7] Mr. Green.

8. Is he good at cooking?　Yes,（ **he**)[8] is.

9. Is he your hero?　（ **Yes**)[9], he is.

10. Where do you want（ **to**)[10] go?　I want to go（ **to**)[11] the amusement park.

11. I want to（ **go**)[12] to the beach.

12. Where is the station?　Go straight.　（ **Turn**)[13] right at the second corner.

13. I'm from London.

14. I'm（ **good**)[14] at singing.

15. What fruit do you like?　（ **I**)[15] like oranges.

16. You can climb the mountain.　It's very beautiful.　Please（ **try**)[16] it.

17. Are you a giraffe?　Yes,（ **I**)[17] am.

18. You can play with the elephants.

19. （ **I**)[18] want to build a house.

20. What is（ **your**)[19] best memory?　My best memory is the school（ **trip**)[20].

21. We went to China in January.

22. What（ **club**)[21] do you want to join?　（ **I**)[22] want to join the cooking club.

23. （ **What**)[23] subject do you want to study hard?　（ **I**)[24] want to study math hard.

24. We（ **have**)[25] many events and activities in junior high school life.

eMET 小学 5 年・6 年総合 (2) 問題

英語の音声を聞きながら, (　　　　) の中に, 4 文字以下 (最大で 4 文字) の英単語を入れてください。

1. What color do you like?　I (　　　　　)^1 blue.

2. Do you like stories?　Yes, (　　　　　)^2 do.

3. Do you have a ruler?　(　　　　　)^3, I don't.

4. He is Bill.　He (　　　　　)^4 swim fast.　He can't run (　　　　　)^5.

5. Who is this?　This is Kate.

6. Where (　　　　　)^6 the racket?　It's by the desk.

7. (　　　　　)^7 she a junior high school student?　Yes, she (　　　　　)^8.

8. She can dance very well.　That's great!

9. Can (　　　　　)^9 fly a kite?　Yes, he (　　　　　)^{10}.

10. You can see it on (　　　　　)^{11} right.

11. This is Miss Davis.　She can swim (　　　　　)^{12} fast.　She is cool. She (　　　　　)^{13} my favorite swimmer.

12. Where do you want to (　　　　　)^{14}?　I want to go to Africa.

13. (　　　　　)^{15} vegetable do you like?　I like tomatoes.

14. Welcome (　　　　　)^{16} my town.

15. My town is beautiful. (　　　　　　)^{17} have a big park.

16. You (　　　　　)^{18} buy good tea.

17. You can visit (　　　　　)^{19} city by boat.

18. Let's sing (　　　　)^{20} song.

19. What did you see? (　　　　　)^{21} saw a lot of temples.

20. I (　　　　)^{22} to see the singer.

21. I want (　　　　)^{23} go to the zoo.

22. What (　　　　)^{24} do you want to join? (　　　　　)^{25} want to join the volleyball club.

23. (　　　　　)^{26} school event do you want to enjoy? I (　　　　)^{27} to enjoy sports day.

24. What do you (　　　　)^{28} to be? I want to (　　　　)^{29} a teacher.

eMET 小学 5 年・6 年総合 (2) 問題 日本語訳

問題英文の日本語訳を確認しよう。

1. 何色が好きですか。私は青色が好きです。

2. あなたは物語が好きですか。はい，好きです。

3. あなたは定規を持っていますか。いいえ，持っていません。

4. 彼はビルです。彼は速く泳ぐことができます。彼は速く走ることができません。

5. これは誰ですか。これはケイトです。

6. ラケットはどこですか。机のそばです。

7. 彼女は中学生ですか。はい。

8. 彼女は上手に踊ることができます。それはすばらしい。

9. 彼は凧をあげることができますか。はい，できます。

10. あなたの右側にそれが見えます。

11. これはデイビスさんです。彼女はとても速く泳ぐことができます。彼女はかっこいいです。彼女は私のお気に入りの水泳選手です。

12. あなたはどこに行きたいですか。私はアフリカに行きたいです。

13. あなたはどんな野菜が好きですか。私はトマトが好きです。

14. 私の町へようこそ。

15. 私の町は美しいです。大きい公園があります。

16. いいお茶が買えますよ。

17. あなたは船でその都市を訪れることができます。

18. 歌を歌いましょう。

19. 何を見ましたか。お寺をたくさん見ました。

20. 私はその歌手を見たいです。

21. 私は動物園に行きたいです。

22. あなたはどのクラブに入りたいですか。私はバレーボールクラブに入りたいです。

23. あなたはどんな学校行事を楽しみたいですか。体育祭を楽しみたいです。

24. あなたは何になりたいですか。先生になりたいです。

eMET 小学 5 年・6 年総合（2）解答

解答付き英文を見ながら，英語の音声をもう一度聞いてみよう。

1. What color do you like?　I（ **like** ）[1] blue.

2. Do you like stories?　Yes,（ **I** ）[2] do.

3. Do you have a ruler?　（ **No** ）[3], I don't.

4. He is Bill.　He（ **can** ）[4] swim fast.　He can't run（ **fast** ）[5].

5. Who is this?　This is Kate.

6. Where（ **is** ）[6] the racket?　It's by the desk.

7. （ **Is** ）[7] she a junior high school student?　Yes, she（ **is** ）[8].

8. She can dance very well.　That's great!

9. Can（ **he** ）[9] fly a kite?　Yes, he（ **can** ）[10].

10. You can see it on（ **your** ）[11] right.

11. This is Miss Davis.　She can swim（ **very** ）[12] fast.　She is cool.　She（ **is** ）[13] my favorite swimmer.

12. Where do you want to（ **go** ）[14]?　I want to go to Africa.

13. （ **What** ）[15] vegetable do you like?　I like tomatoes.

14. Welcome（ **to** ）[16] my town.

15. My town is beautiful.　（ **We** ）[17] have a big park.

16. You（ **can** ）[18] buy good tea.

17. You can visit（ **the** ）[19] city by boat.

18. Let's sing（ **a** ）[20] song.

19. What did you see?　（ **We** ）[21] saw a lot of temples.

20. I（ **want** ）[22] to see the singer.

21. I want（ **to** ）[23] go to the zoo.

22. What（ **club** ）[24] do you want to join?　（ **I** ）[25] want to join the volleyball club.

23. （ **What** ）[26] school event do you want to enjoy?　I（ **want** ）[27] to enjoy sports day.

24. What do you（ **want** ）[28] to be?　I want to（ **be** ）[29] a teacher.

eMET 小学 5 年・6 年総合 (3) 問題

英語の音声を聞きながら, (　　　) の中に, 4 文字以下 (最大で 4 文字) の英単語を入れてください。

1. What do you want for (　　　　　)^1 birthday?   I want a red cap.

2. (　　　　　)^2 day is it today?   It's Friday.

3. When (　　　　　)^3 your birthday?   My birthday is July 4th.

4. Where is (　　　　)^4 book?   You can see it (　　　　　)^5 your left.

5. What can you (　　　　　)^6?   I can run fast.

6. Are (　　　　)^7 good at cooking?   No, I'm not.

7. Where (　　　　)^8 the cat?   It is on (　　　　)^9 box.

8. Where is the fox?   It (　　　　)^{10} in the box.

9. Where do you (　　　　)^{11} to go?   I want to (　　　　)^{12} to Italy.

10. This is Mr. Brown.   He is (　　　　)^{13} firefighter.

11. Who is your best friend?   My (　　　　)^{14} friend is Kate.

12. She is a police officer.

13. We (　　　　)^{15} enjoy fishing.

14. In summer, we have a summer festival.   You (　　　　)^{16} enjoy delicious food.   You can enjoy dancing, too.

15. We (   )¹⁷ an entrance ceremony in April. We don't have

   (   )¹⁸ entrance ceremony in September.

16. Let's cut the cake.

17. (   )¹⁹ am tall.

18. I have long (   )²⁰.

19. Where do dolphins live?   They live in (   )²¹ sea.

20. Where do lions live?   They live (   )²² the savanna.

21. We can read English books in (   )²³ library.

22. Who is your favorite sports player?   My favorite sports player is

   Michael Jordan.

23. (   )²⁴ is a good basketball player.

24. I'm Fred.   I (   )²⁵ to be a scientist.

eMET 小学 5 年・6 年総合 (3) 問題 日本語訳

問題英文の日本語訳を確認しよう。

1. あなたは誕生日に何が欲しいですか。私は赤い帽子が欲しいです。

2. 今日は何曜日ですか。金曜日です。

3. あなたの誕生日はいつですか。私の誕生日は 7 月 4 日です。

4. あなたの本はどこですか。あなたの左側にあります。

5. あなたは何ができますか。私は速く走ることができます。

6. あなたは料理が上手ですか。いいえ，上手じゃありません。

7. 猫はどこですか。箱の上にいます。

8. キツネはどこですか。箱の中です。

9. あなたはどこに行きたいですか。私はイタリアに行きたいです。

10. これはブラウンさんです。彼は消防士です。

11. あなたの一番の友達は誰ですか。私の一番の友達はケイトです。

12. 彼女は警官です。

13. 私たちは釣りを楽しむことができます。

14. 夏には，夏祭りがあります。おいしい食べ物を食べることができます。踊りを楽しむこともできます。

15. 私たちは 4 月に入学式があります。9 月には入学式がありません。

16. ケーキを切りましょう。

17. 私は背が高いです。

18. 私は足が長いです。

19. イルカはどこに住んでいますか。海に住んでいます。

20. ライオンはどこに住んでいますか。サバンナに住んでいます。

21. 私たちは図書館で英語の本を読むことができます。

22. あなたのお気に入りのスポーツ選手は誰ですか。私のお気に入りのスポーツ選手は，マイケル・ジョーダンです。

23. 彼はすばらしいバスケットボール選手です。

24. 私はフレッドです。私は科学者になりたいです。

eMET 小学 5 年・6 年総合（3）解答

解答付き英文を見ながら，英語の音声をもう一度聞いてみよう。

1. What do you want for (**your**)[1] birthday?　I want a red cap.

2. (**What**)[2] day is it today?　It's Friday.

3. When (**is**)[3] your birthday?　My birthday is July 4th.

4. Where is (**your**)[4] book?　You can see it (**on**)[5] your left.

5. What can you (**do**)[6]?　I can run fast.

6. Are (**you**)[7] good at cooking?　No, I'm not.

7. Where (**is**)[8] the cat?　It is on (**the**)[9] box.

8. Where is the fox?　It (**is**)[10] in the box.

9. Where do you (**want**)[11] to go?　I want to (**go**)[12] to Italy.

10. This is Mr. Brown.　He is (**a**)[13] firefighter.

11. Who is your best friend?　My (**best**)[14] friend is Kate.

12. She is a police officer.

13. We (**can**)[15] enjoy fishing.

14. In summer, we have a summer festival.　You (**can**)[16] enjoy delicious food.　You can enjoy dancing, too.

15. We (**have**)[17] an entrance ceremony in April.　We don't have (**an**)[18] entrance ceremony in September.

16. Let's cut the cake.

17. (**I**)[19] am tall.

18. I have long (**legs**)[20].

19. Where do dolphins live?　They live in (**the**)[21] sea.

20. Where do lions live?　They live (**in**)[22] the savanna.

21. We can read English books in (**the**)[23] library.

22. Who is your favorite sports player?　My favorite sports player is Michael Jordan.

23. (**He**)[24] is a good basketball player.

24. I'm Fred.　I (**want**)[25] to be a scientist.

eMET 小学 5 年・6 年総合 (4) 問題

英語の音声を聞きながら, ( ) の中に, 4 文字以下 (最大で 4 文字) の英単語を入れてください。

1. What season do you like?   I ( )^1 summer.

2. How many CDs do you have?   ( )^2 have twenty CDs.

3. How much is this ( )^3?   It's 500 yen.

4. Where is the bookstore?   Go straight for ( )^4 block.

5. Turn left.   You can see ( )^5 on your right.

6. Can you do ( )^6?

7. Why?   I want to eat pizza.

8. ( )^7 do you do on New Year's Day?   I usually ( )^8 cards.

9. What do you want for ( )^9 birthday?   I want a bicycle.

10. What do ( )^{10} want for lunch?   I want a ( )^{11} dog.

11. What would you like?   I'd ( )^{12} pizza.

12. What is this city famous ( )^{13}?   It's famous for its snow festival.

13. We have ( )^{14} Star Festival in July.

14. You can visit the temple today.   It's beautiful.

15. (   )¹⁵ can see the festival in August. It's (   )¹⁶ interesting.

16. Let's go to India.   India is a (   )¹⁷ country.

17. Why do you like India?

18. Are (   )¹⁸ from Mexico?   No, I'm not.

19. We (   )¹⁹ play baseball at the park.

20. In London, (   )²⁰ can ride on a boat (   )²¹ the river. We can see castles, too.

21. (   )²² live in Florida. We have beautiful beaches. We (   )²³ swim in the clear water. We love Florida (   )²⁴ much.

22. Why?   I like my science classes.

23. (   )²⁵ name is Mary White.   I saw a (   )²⁶ of taxis in New York.

24. My favorite memory is the summer (   )²⁷.

eMET 小学 5 年・6 年総合 (4) 問題 日本語訳

問題英文の日本語訳を確認しよう。

1. あなたはどの季節が好きですか。私は夏が好きです。

2. あなたは CD を何枚持っていますか。私は CD を 20 枚持っています。

3. このバッグはいくらですか。500 円です。

4. 本屋はどこですか。1 ブロック直進してください。

5. 左に曲がってください。そうすると，右側に見えます。

6. あなたはこれができますか。

7. なぜですか。ピザが食べたいからです。

8. お正月は何をしますか。私はだいたいトランプをします。

9. 誕生日に何が欲しいですか。自転車が欲しいです。

10. あなたは昼に何が食べたいですか。私はホットドッグが食べたいです。

11. 何にしますか。ピザにします。

12. この都市は何で有名ですか。雪祭りで有名です。

13. 7 月に七夕祭りがあります。

14. 今日そのお寺を訪れることができます。美しいですよ。

15. 8 月にその祭りを見ることができます。とても面白いですよ。

16. インドに行きましょう。インドはすばらしい国です。

17. なぜインドが好きなんですか。

18. あなたはメキシコ出身ですか。いいえ，違います。

19. 私たちは公園で野球をすることができます。

20. ロンドンでは，川で船に乗ることができます。城も見ることができます。

21. 私たちはフロリダに住んでいます。きれいな浜辺があります。澄んだ水の中を泳ぐこと
   ができます。私たちはフロリダが大好きです。

22. なぜですか。理科の授業が好きだからです。

23. 私の名前はメアリー・ホワイトです。私はニューヨークでタクシーをたくさん見ました。

24. 私のお気に入りの思い出は夏のキャンプです。

eMET 小学 5 年・6 年総合 (4) 解答

解答付き英文を見ながら，英語の音声をもう一度聞いてみよう。

1. What season do you like?　I (**like**)¹ summer.

2. How many CDs do you have?　(**I**)² have twenty CDs.

3. How much is this (**bag**)³?　It's 500 yen.

4. Where is the bookstore?　Go straight for (**one**)⁴ block.

5. Turn left.　You can see (**it**)⁵ on your right.

6. Can you do (**this**)⁶?

7. Why?　I want to eat pizza.

8. (**What**)⁷ do you do on New Year's Day?　I usually (**play**)⁸ cards.

9. What do you want for (**your**)⁹ birthday?　I want a bicycle.

10. What do (**you**)¹⁰ want for lunch?　I want a (**hot**)¹¹ dog.

11. What would you like?　I'd (**like**)¹² pizza.

12. What is this city famous (**for**)¹³?　It's famous for its snow festival.

13. We have (**the**)¹⁴ Star Festival in July.

14. You can visit the temple today.　It's beautiful.

15. (**You**)¹⁵ can see the festival in August.　It's (**very**)¹⁶ interesting.

16. Let's go to India.　India is a (**nice**)¹⁷ country.

17. Why do you like India?

18. Are (**you**)¹⁸ from Mexico?　No, I'm not.

19. We (**can**)¹⁹ play baseball at the park.

20. In London, (**we**)²⁰ can ride on a boat (**on**)²¹ the river.　We can see castles, too.

21. (**We**)²² live in Florida.　We have beautiful beaches.　We (**can**)²³ swim in the clear water.　We love Florida (**very**)²⁴ much.

22. Why?　I like my science classes.

23. (**My**)²⁵ name is Mary White.　I saw a (**lot**)²⁶ of taxis in New York.

24. My favorite memory is the summer (**camp**)²⁷.

参考文献

牧秀樹（2018）『The Minimal English Test（最小英語テスト）研究』，開拓社，東京.

Nishida, Hina（2023）*A Study on the elementary Minimal English Test (eMET)*, Bachelor's thesis, Gifu University.

牧　秀樹（まき　ひでき）

　岐阜大学地域科学部シニア教授。1995 年にコネチカット大学にて博士号（言語学）を取得。研究対象は，言語学と英語教育。
　主な著書：*Essays on Irish Syntax*（共著，2011 年），*Essays on Mongolian Syntax*（共著，2015 年），*Essays on Irish Syntax II*（共著，2017 年），『The Minimal English Test（最小英語テスト）研究』（2018 年），『誰でも言語学』，『最小英語テスト（MET）ドリル』〈標準レベル：高校生から社会人〉，〈センター試験レベル〉，『中学生版 最小英語テスト（jMET）ドリル』（以上，2019 年），「英語 monogrammar シリーズ」『関係詞』『比較』『準動詞』『助動詞・仮定法』『時制・相』『動詞』（監修，以上，2020-2021 年），『金言版 最小英語テスト（kMET）ドリル』（2020 年），『これでも言語学—中国の中の「日本語」』，*Essays on Case*（以上，2021 年），『それでも言語学—ヒトの言葉の意外な約束』，『最小日本語テスト（MJT）ドリル』，『最小中国語テスト（MCT）ドリル』，『最小韓国語テスト（MKT）ドリル』（以上，2022 年），『MCT 中国語実践会話—学びなおしとステップアップ 上海出張・日本紹介』（共著，2023 年），『象の鼻から言語学—主語・目的語カメレオン説』（2023 年）［以上，開拓社］，『10 分でわかる！ことばの仕組み』（2023 年，Kindle Direct Publishing）など。

西田　雛（にしだ　ひな）

　岐阜大学地域科学部卒業。在学中，牧秀樹研究室に所属。研究対象は，最小英語テスト小学生版。

小学生版 最小英語テスト（eMET）ドリル

ISBN978-4-7589-2337-8　C0082

著作者	牧　秀樹・西田　雛
発行者	武村哲司
印刷所	日之出印刷株式会社

2023 年 9 月 24 日　第 1 版第 1 刷発行©

〒112-0013　東京都文京区音羽 1-22-16
電話　（03）5395-7101（代表）
振替　00160-8-39587
http://www.kaitakusha.co.jp

発行所　　株式会社　開拓社